C000136053

Thick Richard has been peddling his potty-mouthed punk poetry since the turn of the century. He has supported John Hegley, Kate Tempest, Jerry Sadowitz, The Fall, Arthur Smith and (sort of) Dr. John Cooper Clarke, performed on BBC Radio 4 and presented Radio 6 Music's *Beat of the Day*. He was co-host of *Bang Said the Gun: Manchester* and his one-man show *Swear School* premiered in 2016 before touring nationally.

This is the first time his words have been securely trapped in a book.

the Stuff Nightmares Are Made of

HA HA HA HA HA HA HA HA HA HA HA HA HA HA HA HA HA HA HA HA HA HA HA HA HA

THICK RICHARD
VAUD A VILLAIN

Flapjack Press
flapjackpress.co.uk

Exploring the synergy between performance and the page

Published in 2017 by Flapjack Press, Salford, Gtr Manchester
flapjackpress.co.uk

Reprinted in 2018

ISBN 978-0-9955012-5-6

Drawings by Matthew Duffy
Photographs courtesy of the author

Cover photo by Nathan McDowell
nathanmcdowell.net

Printed by Imprint Digital, Upton Pyne, Exeter, Devon
imprintdigital.com

Thick Richard will not be held responsible for the theft or damage that may occur to
any personal property while reading this.
Thick Richard are not a religious organisation.
No solid evidence exists relating Thick Richard to the deaths of any major celebrities
in the past 4 years.
Thick Richard cannot spell their own name.
Thick Richard will not help you lose weight as part of a calorie controlled diet and
may contain traces of nut or nut oils.
Thick Richard will not change your life for the better.
Thick Richard cannot remember 1998 of the last half of 1999.
Thick Richard know where you live.
Thick Richard will not use G.M. products, canned laughter or Tip-x.
Thick Richard saw nothing!
Thick Richard will agree to appear naked, providing the price is negotiable.
Any similarities between characters in this book to persons living or dead are purely
intentional.
Thick Richard take the fifth amendment.
Thick Richard deny all the above information to be true.

**For best results
read out loud**

CONTENTS

III : The Sound Of One Fan Clapping 84

'Scum of the Earth' was first published in *Wordlife: an anthology,* 2016.

'Love in a Sling' was first published in *Dreams That Money Can Buy, vol. 4,* 2006.

'The Waste Paper Updates' was first published in 2015.

I SUPPOSE THE NICE THING TO DO WHEN YOUVE WRITTEN A BOOK IS TO DEDICATE IT TO YOUR KIDS OR YOUR MUM + DAD. I WILL NOT BE DEDICATEING THIS BOOK TO JACOB, LOUIE, SUE OR BRIAN. SOZ! I WILL NOT ALLOW SUCH HORID THOUGHTS, NAUGHTY WORDS, REVOLTING IMIGARY + BITTER DARK HUMOUR, THAT PROBABLY ONLY I FIND FUNNY, BE PRINTED IN YOUR NAMES. I HAVE TOO MUCH LOVE + RESPECT FOR YOU. YOUR BETTER THAN THIS. SORRY X

I SHALL BE DEDICATEING THIS BOOK TO EMMA X
SHE DOSE DESERVE SUCH WORDS, + I KNOW SHE FINDS THEM FUNNY TOO.

I SHALL BE DEDICATEING THIS BOOK TO PHILIP, THE ONE MAN FAN CLUB, WHO ACTUALLY SUGESTED A LOT OF THESE WORDS X

+ I SHALL BE DEDICATEING THIS BOOK TO HELEN, THE LAST PERSON ON EARTH WHO SHOULD HEAR SUCH HORRIBLE THINGS, BUT HAD TO HEAR IT AS SHE TYPED IT ALL OUT (FOR YOUR BENIFIT. OTHER WISE YOUD BE READING A WHOLE BOOK IN THIS DYSLEXIC CHIKEN SCRACH!)
ALL MY LOVE X

THE BEAST OF BAGULEY
(and other urban myths)

I was born on the second of January 1979 exactly one month to the day before Sid Vicious died, which means I just about qualify to remember punk rock.

When growing up in Manchester my dad's side of the family lived in Wythenshawe and my mum's side lived in Stretford. The area that links these two parts of south Manchester is called Sale and that's where we lived.

The first house I lived in was in Northern Moor where the north side of Wythenshawe meets Sale Moor. A few years back Sarah Ferguson declared Northern Moor the most deprived area in England. (It wasn't. It was bad, but there are far worse.) She went with a TV documentary crew to build a youth club for the area and the local youths showed their appreciation by shooting bullets at it till it collapsed. Fergie and the camera crew fled and are yet to return.

Wythenshawe has a well-earned Wild West reputation. After the post-war population boom it became the largest council estate in Europe and the rats maze of identical streets, windowless pubs and bulletproof shops can seem terrifying and infinite to a lost stranger. However, if you catch it in the right light, it is actually one of the prettiest parts of Manchester (tower blocks, motorways and people sheds aside). The houses are actually quite large with front and back gardens, the roads are broad, and there are leafy trees and communal greens on every street. Nevertheless, it's a world class shithouse!

In my early twenties I took a gap year in Macclesfield, then known as "Smacklesfield" due to the local devotion to the intravenous drug. In the early '70s the area had become so inbred the council moved families from the overpopulated area of Wythenshawe to Mac, who brought with them fresh DNA and various heroin contacts. The Manchester to London train used to stop at Macclesfield and I was told if you looked to the countryside on the right-hand side of the train as you approached the station you could sometimes see kangaroos hopping about the fields.

The rumours of wild foreign animals roaming the English countryside has some truth back from the days of the upper classes moving abroad to teach Johnny Foreigner how to be a gentleman. The entitlement of money and a proper education meant there were no quarrels in them bringing home a "big cat" or two. Only when the butler is mauled to death by a full-grown leopard would they have to sadly set it free to fend for itself through the British winter. No one knows how many survived.

In the early '90s a similar story was whispering round Manchester that a "big cat" had been spotted around Wythenshawe. Usually English "wild animal" stories are just tossed into the urban myth pile without a second thought. But "The Beast of Baguley", as it became known, held more weight because, with Wythenshawe's reputation, coming face to face with a jaguar in broad daylight on the streets of Baguley seems entirely plausible.

"Why do you think we all carry guns, dickhead?"

But, before the neighbourhood was filled with Jeeps packed with cider-swilling youths shooting anything that moved, the rumours were disproved. One of the area's more heroic head-cases set off to "bang that jaguar out", but as he approached it in a corner of Wythenshawe park he found on closer inspection that it was just a black bin bag caught in the branches of a tree.

I never liked Wythenshawe (don't tell them that I said that, they scare the shit out of me!). To call yourself a Wythenshawe lad requires qualifications. They have earned blood badges, tallied of prison years with scars. I grew up round there but was always whisked off to safety before it kicked-off proper. Like my Uncle Tommy's wedding. Even at the age of five I could tell things were getting a bit hairy as all us kids were stuck in a taxi just before Tommy's brand-new brother-in-law pulled out a machete. A guy lost an arm. It made the *Manchester Evening News*. "Machete Massacre at Wythenshawe Wedding" the front page said. Who takes a machete to a wedding?!

None of my cousins know I grew up to be a poet. And I'd like it to stay that way. I come from a long line of shit thieves. A laughable Manc Mafia family of disorganised crime. My dad never said anything but he always seemed a bit confused by his specky skinny son who couldn't throw a punch. When I was fourteen I stayed out all night on a cider binge with my mate. We were picked up by the police at 4 in the morning for carrying an offensive weapon. My dad looked furious when he opened the door half-awake in his vest and pants but when he saw the copper with his hand on my shoulder a gleeful smirk flashed over his face. I walked in head hung but instead of the furious bollocking I anticipated he threw the knife in the kitchen bin and chuckled "get to bed you bloody idiot". I had made him proud and I therefore felt no reason to pursue the family's young offender tradition any further.

When I was six we moved two streets further into Sale to a house that had just been built. I lived there till I was eleven and in that time they didn't really build many more houses, so for five years I lived on a building site.

[Parents: if possible try not to live on a building site, they are even more dangerous than you think and your children WILL play on them.]

[Kids: playing on building sites is the best fun you will ever have and if the opportunity arises I cannot recommend it highly enough. It's like a wacky warehouse but free, there're no rules and there's a real risk of dying. Half-built houses you can have to yourself, loads of sand everywhere, breeze-blocks as big as your head (but light enough to throw at each other), games of hide and seek that last the entire six-week holiday and never get boring.]

There was this huge pit we called "the gorge". It was at least fifteen feet deep and bigger than a football pitch with a swamp at the bottom; easily deep enough to drown an unconscious child. We were always pushing each other in it or falling off the edge of it. I remember one time playing "Ghostbusters" in an almost-finished house; I was stood on the roof and my mate jumped out, frightening me and I fell off. Luckily I landed on a pile of sand,

13

knackered my ankle but still laughing. Great fun. I can't believe none of us died. Also, my family must have lifted enough gear to build at least another two houses so we all enjoyed living there.

I was a filthy cretin as a child, usually covered in mud. I was fond of burying myself. Somewhere in the building site I would hide beneath the ground and when someone would walk past I would emerge from the earth singing Michael Jackson's 'Thriller'. I thought the look of disgust on their faces was from seeing a real zombie but they were probably just disgusted in me. Good times!

Good times for me anyway, this was the late '80s and everybody else was getting shafted. In our house politics was as much a thing as the walls and floor. MPs would come to the area and debates would be held at decided houses. I remember terrified politicians standing by the fireplace trying to talk to a house full of shouting grown-ups whilst me and the other kids watched from the kitchen eating biscuits. Swearing and throwing things seemed to be acceptable when Thatcher was on the telly. Before we got a telly an evening's entertainment for me and my mum would be watching my dad and my sister argue politics and religion despite the fact they both agreed on most topics. We'd sit on the couch rolling our eyes as they locked antlers and I subconsciously took notes on the language and techniques of the aggressive dance that I'd later build a career on. In 1990 my dad helped organise four coaches to London for the poll tax riots. We didn't see dad for a while after that. So me, my mum and my sister went to live with my grandad in Stretford.

I love Stretford. I've lived here most of my life and it's where I consider home. It's moody and gloomy but there's an upbeat "just-got-out-of-prison-this-morning" jollity to it. Stretford seems to be drunk most of the time. It looks like *Coronation Street*, but with the *EastEnders* storylines and there seems to be more sky here than elsewhere in Manchester.

"E'ar, yo!"

The traditional Mancunian greeting yelled down the street at me with aggressive familiarity.

"E'ar, yo! Got a spare cig?"

And as I give them a cigarette I tell them that "E'ar, yo" is actually Latin for "excuse me" and they walk off without so much as a thank you.

When I was fourteen we moved to Cheadle Hulme. Cheadle is where Manchester meets the middle-class Greater Manchester big money. Bramhall, Wilmslow, Alderley Edge. Footballer Land. Where Ken Barlow *really* lives. It's said this part of England houses more millionaires per square mile than anywhere else in the country. But the richer millionaires would own more land so there'd be fewer per square mile in posher areas. If you get what I mean.

Greater Manchester and the Cheshire Set must meet somewhere and the boundary is Edgeley, Stockport, home of Stockport County FC. A right dump. When the Southerners mock the Mancs for wearing flat caps and eating tripe on the outside toilet it's Edgeley that they're thinking of. And that's where we lived, right on the border of Stockport's armpit and the strongest Conservative seat in Manchester.

I hadn't really been aware of class till I lived there. The place had an ugly working-class snootiness. Puffed-up naïve Tories proud of their postcode because they shared it with the big houses three and a half miles away, stubbornly ignoring the fact they live just a ten minute walk from Stockport town centre. A diameter no one should be proud of. There were just as many scallys (who hated me) and vandalism and abandoned cars and dog shit than anywhere else in Greater Manchester but this was Cheadle so it was different, not like scummy Wythenshawe with its Tudoresque architecture and resilient community spirit. Cheadle was a terrible place to be a teenager. I spent as little time there as I could and only really went home to eat. No bus went there after 6pm which would mean a two mile walk from Parrs Wood, always better than the ten minute walk from Stockport. I left home at the first opportunity at seventeen.

Last time I found myself in Edgeley it was a match day. Everyone on the street was pissed. A large man walked towards me with a four year old girl on his shoulders. I don't know what

15

they were talking about but as they passed me I heard him tell her, "Well, if any copper comes near me, man knows he's going to get knocked the fuck out.". It's just a better class of person round there.

The rise of the working-class capitalist...

"Doctor, doctor, there's something wrong with my eyes! I can only see the worst in people!"

"Hmm, yes. I think I know what the problem is. You've looked at the sun for too long and now you're a Tory."

"Well what can you do for me?"

"Not much I'm afraid. You see, a few years ago working-class pride was strengthened by the fact that we could look down on the bigoted ruling classes for their inability to understand equality. Minorities united makes a majority and they hated us for that. Their plan was to place Conservative views amongst the working classes to divide us, disguised as a tabloid newspaper for the people, and you ate it all up didn't you? And now you blame everybody else for your problems. Immigrants, gays, foreigners, women, teenagers, the disabled, the elderly, the young, even people just as poor as you are, because it makes you feel you have an upper-handed opinion and feel you're on the winning team. And since you lot just sold off the NHS it's now going to cost you £15 for me to tell you this. Good day!"

One good memory of that place was the '96 election. It was a hot day and we'd spent the afternoon drinking in the back garden talking about how Labour would definitely win (things can only get better, eh Tony?) In the evening we went off to vote. A shiny-faced Tory boy stood at the door of the polling station with a huge ridiculous blue rosette pined to his lapel like an elephant's arsehole.

"And I trust you'll be voting Conservative today," he simpered smugly.

My dad lent towards him, their noses almost touching.

"FUCK OFF!" he bellowed.

Well things didn't get better did they. They got worse. The angry young men got tired of fighting and became embarrassed old men, shamed by getting sold out by "new" Labour. The politicians hid. Never again would they be made to venture into the estates and have to debate face-to-face with their people. The working-class capitalists borrowed so much invisible money to keep up their pretences that many became *sub*-working-class capitalists indebted so far into the negatives it would become their grandchildren's inheritance. Issues became so complicated it felt like what was being discussed was none of our business and many people started to shy away from political debate through fear of coming across as stupid. Then the confusing issues just became boring issues. The internet had evidence to back up every side of every argument so everyone fell into the false security trap that they were all in the right. Communities stopped communicating, generation gaps grew leaving room for bad ideas to breed and now racism is an actual political opinion. We've never been so divided and it all happened right under our noses.

I moved back to Northern Moor in my early thirties. It's a sour haunted place that would have Fergie waking up screaming. Its political edge grew blunt long ago. The thugs of the neighbourhood used to seem like Robin Hoods, their disobedience was righteous and justified, their tempers were taught but focused on the right targets. Built for a fight if needs be but perfectly capable of letting their words do the dirty work. They'd never be able to save up for a holiday but the money could always be found to march on London, demand answers and shake Tony Benn's hand. These days they keep themselves to themselves and prey on one another. Quiet. Invisible. Forgotten. Obedient.

And so now we all just hope for the rumours to start spreading again of the "wild beasts" of the past. The animals of passionate anger who would never have let this happen, returning to prowl the streets again, keeping the territory safe from harm. Watching the pack and planning attacks to keep the real wolves away...

...and other urban myths.

Book One

VAUDAVILLAINS

There used to be two Thick Richard. Sounds weird I know, but Richard isn't my name, nor is it the character name of some alter-ego. Thick Richard is the title of a double act that was me and a mad man called Bob Moyler.

As teenagers me and Bob were in a few bands together which I wrote the lyrics for and Bob organised the gigs. We contributed nothing performance-wise except getting wasted on stage. Eventually the singers and the musicians quit the bands, which just left me and Bob. Then Bob, in a moment of stubborn genius, thought it would be a good idea to continue performing the songs without the band! We would basically carry on booking gigs as what could arguably be the worst band in the world and then just go on stage and shout at the audience and, to our utter horror, people enjoyed it!

It turned out however that Bob's ground-breaking new art form hadn't just been done before, it was actually the oldest art form in the history of mankind and we had inadvertently become *poets* by accident. But the poetry scene seemed unnerved and disgusted by us and the feeling was mutual. Preferring to think of ourselves as "The worst band in the world" me and Bob performed together as Thick Richard for seven years at band nights, comedy clubs, music festivals, squat raves, vaudevilles and quite a few family fun days.

So you see, this is all Bob's fault.

This chapter is a collection of stuff me and Bob performed together as Thick Richard. To experience the true atmosphere these pieces should be heard in wash down five pills with a half-litre of vodka, go to a bar in Manchester wearing a string vest and a giant papier-mâché snowman's head, stand on a table and scream these poems whilst waving a replica gun about and then fall off the table landing on the back of your head.

This chapter is dedicated to Bob Moyler, wherever he may be. I seem to remember he became a Morris Dancer or something. There's a rumour going round that I killed and ate Bob to gain his knowledge. I even heard one story that he moved to Glasgow with his girlfriend and child and he now performs experimental theatre with a sex robot called Roomba.

My friends and family deny any knowledge of Bob's existence and are desperately pushing me to accept the fact that he was a figment of my imagination that only I could see.

BAD JACK

Part 1: Bad Jack

I shot Bob Hoskins in the back of a cab
I shot Joe Pesci in the back of the head
I shot Tony Montana
I shot JR
I am the man with the prosthetic arm

I shot Dennis Hopper in a caravan
I shot Kevin Spacey in the kitchen
I shot Charles Hale
I shot Van Cleef
I shot Michael Caine on the beach

Bad Jack took me in his sweaty palm
And promised he'd make me a success
He told me that money talks
But not to believe a word it says
Shop shutters slammed like guillotines
As Bad Jack approached the vicinity
Apocalyptic graffiti
Written in red on corrugated steel with no initials

Part 2: Who Shot the Rabbit?

Playground rampage
Jack got drunk
Screaming blue murder
And singing this song
But that's not a toy gun
Jack you got it wrong
Bullets for drumsticks
Bodies for drums

Bullets for drumsticks
Bodies for drums
Because music ain't shit without war and drumsticks
Bullets for drumsticks
Bodies for drums

Who shot the rabbit?

Carmel's on the corner
Wishing she was never born
But I guess it's tough luck
She turns 26 next month
And Carmel's looking thin
She's got a skeleton like scaffolding
Trying to hold her insides in
I heard her rooting through the bathroom cabinet
Searching for razors and sleeping tablets
I bust down the door
She's up to no good
Slumped in the bathtub covered in blood
Pinned to her back was a ransom note
Oh no the whole commode's covered in bullet holes

Who shot the rabbit?

Did I write this song
When I was drunk?
That ain't necessarily so
If I wrote this
When I was pissed
I wouldn't remember one word I wrote
And if I could hear you singing
I'd sing along with you
But I can't hear you sing a fucking thing
And so I sing alone

Part 3: Bad Jack

...And Bad Jack said...

Can I trust you?
Because if you will not be true
I will have to beat you black and blue
And if you tell anyone my name
You'll never speak another word again
So don't go running to the police
Because they couldn't catch chlamydia
Never mind a fucking thief
Couldn't keep a pet cat
Never mind the peace
And they won't catch Bad Jack
And that's a fucking promise

Part 4: Mancunian Way

You see Bad Jack standing outside the shops
With his tracksuit bottoms tucked in his socks
I thought Reeboks were supposed to feel soft
But you find out they're not when they're stamping on your face
But hey, that's the Mancunian way

Because they don't give a fuck about you or me
Some people will kill for what they need
And if you think that out on those streets
That there's some kind of pride amongst thieves
Then I'm telling you
You'd better open your eyes
You've seen *Goodfellas* too many times
Will you still feel safe
When you're standing on your own
With a drug-crazed cut-throat razor at your throat
And his hands are in your pocket

And he's after your wallet
And he's laughing
"What the fuck are you going to do about it?"
Well what are you going to do?
Are you going to fight back?
Do you really think Big Brother's watching your back?
Yeah they might catch him on CCTV
But they'll also see you dying on screen
Or maybe you'll stand up to him
Teach the prick a lesson
The bittersweet taste of his own medicine
And end up standing on the wrong side of court
Getting done by a criminal
For criminal assault
Congratulations
Hoo(fucking)ray
You've just found the Mancunian way

Because it's not just gangsters that live in Manchester
Some people live in fear
But for them street life's not something to learn
It's something to preserve
And they say it's ok and you'll get used
To the mindless violence and verbal abuse
And the whites fight the blacks
And the reds fight the blues
Football's got fuck all to do with
Which team wins and which team loses
It's just who gets their heads kicked in by the hooligans
And who gets their heads kicked in by the police
They're not fighting for peace as they fight on the streets
And as they put up the barricades
Halfway through the Commonwealth Games
I felt ashamed but I'm afraid to say
That's the Mancunian way

SOMEBODY'S BABY

Based on the song 'John James' by Toots and the Maytals.

Nice one Simon
Standing outside
With a fist full of nickels
And a toothpaste tie
You were caught in the corner of a club you know
You were looking suspicious and acting stoned
But you don't know anyone who supplies coke
So you just cut a box of bleach with a tub of glucose
Eventually these two guys come along
You don't know 'em too good but you've seen 'em around
So you sell 'em a gram, got £65
They dance off and you roll up the notes
But then they caught you later on in the toilets
They kicked down the cubicle door and said
They found it was bleach that you'd sold 'em
When the cartilage inside their noses dissolved
And now they want their money back
But you don't have it
So they smash your kneecaps
And steal your jacket
The bastards
You won't be going back to that club Simon
You wake up under artificial lights
Your legs are in splinters
There's a drip by your side
You're thinking
Hang on, where am I?
You're barely alive in the MRI
So you run down the corridors with a drip in your arm
And you slide down a drainpipe into a car park
And you hotwire a transit van

To see if you can
Get the hell out of this shitty town
So you're driving down the road
In a van you've just stolen
You're still dressed in your hospital robes
And there's police car sirens
On the horizon
Chasing you for your reckless driving
And then you realise
Shit, I can't drive
The van goes through a bus stop and rolls over on its side
So nice one Simon
Trapped inside a van
Your face went through the windscreen
And you've severed both your hands
And what goes through your head
As they pronounce you dead
And return you to the hospital that you just fucking left?
Nice one Simon
I guess they were right
They said when you were 16
You'll be dead by 25

Daddy's in a stolen car
Daddy's in a stolen car

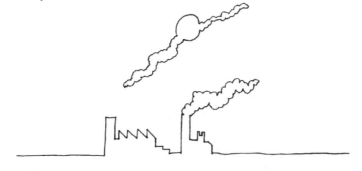

Gorgeous horns and tin violins
Comfortable drums and rubberband bass strings
Slap your ears like an angry hand
Lift you up and drop you down
The music sets the mood
Atmosphere thick as the glutinous soup
As sickly sweet as the tiramisu
As spicy as the devilled sauce
This stuff burns far hotter than love

Tabasco

Dressed in expensive threads that don't fit
His shoes step with a handsome click
Marinated in aftershave
Shakes her hand like he's emptying an ashtray
Conversation came rarely and even when it did
It sounds like their words were being read from a script
And my god those words must weigh a ton
Chokes your throat and twists your tongue
Knocks you sick down to the stomach
Milk of Magnesia won't do no good
This stuff burns far hotter than love

Tabasco

She's a little black cloud hanging over your head
You're the anchor on this relationship wreck
You high-wired peacock prided
Four-eyed intellectual type
She's blonde and she has more fun
Than the brunette bimbo that she stole you from
All of a sudden you're a volcanic eruption

Half-temper half-tantrum
Fuelled by a fire inside your gut
This stuff burns far hotter than love

Tabasco

Oh no! What a sickening blow
She leaves you standing in the middle of the road
With the weight of the whole world on your shoulders
And a white wine and soda
All over your coat
She told you to get stuffed
And that's fair enough
This stuff burns far hotter than love

Tabasco!

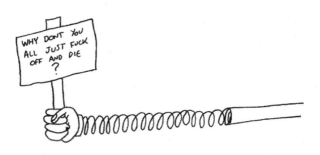

PLYMOUTH GIN

To the tune of 'Opium Tea' by Nick Cave.

Postcards from the edge
Postcards from under the table babe
See the confused look on my face
As I struggle to remember your name
I couldn't give a toss about the North
I'm packing my bags and heading down South
I'm going to swap all of the tea in China
For all of the gin in Plymouth
Do you believe that Jesus Christ
Could turn water into wine
Well if so
I've got no time for him
Coz all I drinks is Plymouth Gin
The loan sharks are circling
The bailiffs are closing in
But it's easy not to give a fuck about a thing
When you're sipped to the tits on mother's ruin
So if you couldn't really give two fucks
Pull a chair up
Grab yourself a cup
Grow fins
Jump right in
Learn to swim in a bottle full of Plymouth Gin
I can hardly find the time to party
I've been sipping G&Ts from nine to five
And I haven't had a thing to eat since last Friday
Except for ninety-five slices of lime
I said Plymouth
Not Vermouth
Don't drown my drink in orange juice
Listen Sonny Jim
It's a mortal sin

I even boil my eggs in Plymouth Gin
Too drunk for lunch
They call me obnoxious
Just because I fill my drink to the top of my cup
Well talk about stating the bleeding obvious
I'm so spannered I can barely stand up
And I've been told to quit
Doctor's orders
So now I'm mixing my drink with a little Rose's lime cordial
And as I sit here
Wondering whether that's a good thing
I sip from a teacup full of Plymouth Gin

MEDICINE BALL

The shit that killed Elvis was three feet long
Broke his pelvis
Solid as a rock
Jet black
Piping hot
The shit that killed Elvis weighed a quarter of a ton
I like my rockstars dead
With an orange in their mouth
Handcuffed to a bed
Choking to death on their own vomit
Could be drugs
Could be a ham sandwich
I don't care
It makes them sound better
I like my rockstars dead
Found weighing a thousand pounds
On the toilet
Dragged back by a life support
Sobering up on a hospital ward
With a beer gut like a medicine ball
Sod that
I'd rather you went with a smile
Stood on the stage drugged up to the eyeballs
You want to see The Big Bopper
Buddy Holly or Aaliyah
It's more likely pigs might fly
I wonder if Lisa Left Eye Lopes's
Left eye's started decomposing yet?
Happy-Go-Lucky Hip Hop
Fuck off
I like my rockstars dead
I don't care if you have to kill yourselves
Like Kurt Cobain
Just ask Richie Edwards

The suicide is painless
Everything's going to be alright
Everything's going to be alright
Well I think Bob Marley lied
Why?
Because he died
Everything wasn't alright
And talk about living on borrowed time
I just heard Phil Collins is playing live
And I'm pretty pissed off that he hasn't died
I like my rockstars dead!

In loving memory of David boo-hoo-ie, Leonard going, the artist formerly know as "the artist formerly known as Prince" and the artist formerly known as Prince Buster, Pete burns! and Keith "art is long, life is short" Emerson. That's the way I like it baby, I didn't want Lemmy to live forever. 2016 wasn't good enough for me I LIKE MY ROCKSTARS DEAD xxx

You can't eat nothing but your fingernails
Because you can't stand the wait
It seems like you've been smoking for all these years
Just rehearsing for this one day
And when push came to shove
It pushed you so hard
It bowled you right over onto your arse
And now you're spitting and dribbling and trying to talk
With a mouthful of word salad

We know the universe is infinite
But you also know that knowledge isn't
So it's time to take dictation
Try and write down every word that I say
Because you want to sound smarter than the next man
But slow down son
This is no competition
Try to kick back and relax
While you're chewing the fat
You're trying to talk
With a mouthful of word salad

You bit off more than you can chew
Now you're trying to eat your own words
It looks like you've spilt **ALPHABETTI SPAGHETTI**
All down the front of your shirt
And you're opening a can of worms with each word
My god it's making you mad
You're trying to fit your foot in your heart
In a mouthful of word salad

And I don't want to know what's under that overcoat
You're as explosive as a sleeping Doberman...

MAD DOG MAD DOG!
YOU CAN'T ESCAPE!
ALL THE WINDOWS ARE LOCKED WITH PAINT!
THERE'S A PADLOCK ON THE FIRE ESCAPE
AND A MAD DOG AT THE END OF A CHAIN!
SO GET YOUR KICKS BEFORE THIS WHOLE
SHITHOUSE GOES UP IN FLAMES!
SEE MY EXPRESSION CHANGE
AS I GNAW MY WAY THROUGH THIS CHAIN
AIM FOR YOUR JUGULAR VEIN
AND BITE THAT SMILE RIGHT OFF YOUR FACE!
I'M A MOTHER-FUCKING MAD DOG!
A RAGING PIT-BULL IN A CHINA SHOP
WIELDING A FURY LIKE A BASEBALL BAT!
THIS MUSIC MAKES YOU WANT TO PAINT YOUR
BEDROOM BLACK!
ONCE BITTEN!
TWICE SHY!
MY BARK ISN'T WORSE THAN MY BITE!
I'M A CHIPPED-TOOTHED
SHARP-TONGUED
MOTHER-FUCKING MAD DOG!
LOOK AT THE SIZE OF MY MOUTH!
BUILT LIKE A CONCRETE SHITHOUSE
WITH A BARBED WIRE MUZZLE WRAPPED AROUND IT!
YOU THINK I SHOULD THROW IN THE TOWEL
BUT WHAT YOU THINK AND WHAT I KNOW
ARE TWO COMPLETELY DIFFERENT THINGS!
SO TALK ALL YOU LIKE COZ I'M NOT LISTENING!
I'M JUST CHEWING OFF MY OWN TONGUE!
I'M JUST A FOAMING
DRIBBLING
RABID-RIDDEN
FLEA-BITTEN
MOTHER-FUCKING MAD DOG!

Has someone put something in your drink?
Some kind of laxative
Verbal diarrhoea mate
You're talking shit
A colourful language a bit like sick
You better stop blabbing that mouth about
Or you'll get a dose that you won't come down from
You'd better keep that half-brick in your hand
Or else something's gonna happen
Make you wish you had
All of a sudden you start to gag
You tried to cover your mouth with your hand
Too bad lad
You dropped down dead
Choking on a mouthful of word salad

PANDA BARE

YOU SHOULDN'T CALL THE DOCTOR
IF YOU CAN'T AFFORD THE PILLS

*Written to the tune of 'You Shouldn't Call the Doctor (If You Can't
Afford the Bills)' by Dr Feelgood.*

I sold my soul for rock and roll
Twenty Marlboro Lights and a microphone
Half a pint of Jack Daniels and coke
And I changed my name to Mud by deed poll
I swapped my girlfriend for a ticket to London
And a suitcase full of duty paid fags
But I managed to swap her back
For a backpack full of pornographic mags
Hypochondriac
I've got it bad
Dr. Bob came round with his medicine bag
When the symptoms started I thought it was a joke
Now I'm lying in bed with a bowl of chicken soup
It started with me tapping my feet
It started in a taxi ride and ended in a fight
And by the time they found me at the end of the night
I was hid behind the jukebox
Crying my eyes out
So take up thy stethoscope and walk
Listen to the beating of my heart
There's only one way you're going to make it stop
You're going to have to prescribe the strongest medicine you've got
You tried to join in but you broke your arm
Standing in the graveyard scratching your arse
Clutching a lyric sheet with a clenched fist
You've got to treat this shit like the bitch it is
The band were in a rage
When we clambered on stage
We sounded like Chas 'n' Dave on a bad day
And I've never realised that air guitar
Was so closely related to heart failure

So when the palpitations start
Listen to the beating of your heart
There's only one way you're going to make it stop
Dr. Bob
"WHAT?"
Tell them what you've got
"I've got two shots of punk rock
One dose of soul
25 milligrams of rock and roll
Wash it all down with a vodka and coke
And maybe lay off the techno for a month or so
And if the symptoms continue to persist
Milk and alcohol is all that I can suggest"
They say you shouldn't keep your friends
As close as your enemies
Well Bob's not my friend
He's my chemist
And he prescribed me an antibiotic
For an illness that I haven't even got
Tap your feet
Grind your teeth

Don't panic when your heart skips a beat
It's just the palpitations
It's all in your imagination
Your mind playing tricks again
I've got a gaping hole in my memory
I've been poisoned
Dr. Bob's got the remedy
"Quick, eat a couple of these"
What will they do?
"I don't know, let's see"
Move like a wet towel
Bones of rock
Stomach like a bagpipe tied in a knot
Silence is a buzzsaw ringing in my ears
My mind is a jigsaw bits and pieces

I couldn't look more fucked if I tried
I can only open one eye
My muscles spasm with little orgasms
Amphetamine
Trampoline
Straight back up again
God opens up Heaven's gate
Sticks his hand out for me to shake
He sees my pupils dilate
And he tells me to go take a fucking hike
Coz this is the Devil's chemist
And Heaven is an empty place
The Devil's chemist is overrun
The streets are empty coz the air is poisoned
I need comfort
I need tons of it
I don't care which direction it comes from
I just need that social walking stick
Security blanket
Wrap myself up in it
Well this trend better go out of fashion quick
Or else something really bad's gonna happen kids
Because when I lose control
I hit 100 miles an hour
It's like hitting a brick wall
At 100 miles an hour
So when you're in the grips of disease
You shouldn't worry about the medical fees
Blessed relief
Get me a priest
My temperature rises to 100 degrees
Because if it really gets you it can kill
Can't sit still
Still feel ill
Feel more ruff than Cruella DeVille
Well you shouldn't call the Doctor if you can't afford the pills

TOUGH LOVE

I couldn't pay my rent
I had to sell my body
But I didn't make a penny
Because nobody wants me
Oh dear
What are you going to do?
You're wearing high-heeled shoes
You've got the rent boy blues
You've got a room with a view of an outside loo
And a hole in the window which the wind blows through
Bite marks in your pillow
A faded tattoo
And physical abuse from the rent boy blues
And your eyes can't hide the cries of surprise
As you find that some guys
Are of quite some size
Some customers try to be nice
But most like tough love
And you have to oblige
Tough love
I guess life's just like that
Now you shut the fuck up and arch your back
Because if you choose not to follow the rules
You'll feel the wrath of the rent boy blues
Because your pimp's not one to be messed with
If you show love he'll show respect
Once a month he'll pay your rent
But when a John walks in you'd better do as he says
Christ
I bet you wish you'd attended school
Instead of being paid for the rent boy blues
So when you're found bound and gagged in a bin bag

Let's pray they can't contact your mum and dad
Your arm pokes out where the bin bag's ripped
Your arse still drips with cuckoo spit
The police won't even flinch when they find you
Because you're just a born loser
With the rent boy blues

YOU KNOW WHEN YOU THROW YOUR DEAD GOLDFISH IN THE TOILET + FLUSH IT AWAY. + YOU STAND WHACHING IT GO ROUND + DOWN + DOWN + ROUND. WELL, I FEEL JUST LIKE THAT GOLDFISH.

THE JOKE THAT NO ONE GETS

Sixty years old
Dripping with gold
Rings on his fingers and gout in his toes
Security guards wherever he goes
And it's not exactly like he needs them
He stands at six foot three
Fat cigar and sweetcorn teeth
He has to be seen to be believed
He's the king of comedy and this is his patch
He says

> *"My mother-in-law is so fat*
> *That she broke the branches on the family tree*
> *I've got diabetes and so has she*
> *So don't even think about heckling me kid*
> *I've been in this business since it was all trees"*

You cracked a bad egg
You cracked a joke that no one gets
A joke that no one could forget
The joke that Bob Monkhouse rejected

You heard it down the pub
You lost three pints of blood
Spent two weeks in traction with writer's block
The joke that's as subtle as a fucking headbutt
You had to snatch to catch your breath
The joke that no one gets

It's the way you tell 'em
The taste of bitter lemon
The smell of parmesan
The sound of breaking glass
And that punchline
Was enough to make a
40 year old man cry
Made a Blackpool pier capsize
Made a nearby church catch fire
It made a girl in a three year old coma die
Tommy Cooper took it on the chest
The joke that no one gets

The first time I told it
The lenses in my glasses broke
Felt sick to the back teeth
Had toothache for two weeks
I wish I'd bought the house down
And I was trapped inside it
The art of comedy is...

Time wasn't on our side
Everyone in hearing distance
Took offence
All thanks to the joke that no one gets

So let's have a big clap for the next act
He doesn't like women and he doesn't like blacks
And he doesn't like Pakis and he doesn't like Japs
And he doesn't like the Jews and he doesn't like Krauts
But he loves his mother
And that's what counts
R.E.S.P.E.C.T.
D.I.V.O.R.C.E.
Take my wife...
Please, take my wife
And tell me why I've married somebody that I don't like
Why don't I file for a divorce
Why's it so bleeding grim up North
I'm going to take the South by storm
And America isn't going to know what's hit 'em
International next best thing
You know like I said I like my rockstars dead
Well present company excepted
I realise you're not Jimmy Hendrix
But that doesn't make you any exception
So you just keep on sipping those brandies
And eating three black puddings a day
And we'll be sitting on the back row waiting to do our set
Dancing on your grave
And until the day
That we get paid
Think twice before you complain
About us two getting shit-faced on stage
Because nobody wants to be famous nowadays

WE'RE ALL GOING ON A BUNGLE HUNT

I'm going on a Bungle hunt
I'm gonna go on a Bungle hunt
I'm gonna get me a fucking Bungle
I'm gonna lay down some Coco Pops as bait
Hide behind that little cardboard wall and wait
And hopefully the bear trap will be powerful enough
To snap Bungle's fucking arm in half
Then I'm gonna chop off his head
Stick it above my fireplace
Skin him
Clean him
And use him as a fucking rug
I'm gonna get me a fucking Bungle

Then I'm gonna get me a fucking Emu
I'm gonna get Michael Parkinson to hold him in a headlock
Then I'm gonna pluck him
Cook him
And fucking eat him
Rod Hull just fell past the window!
I'm gonna get me a fucking Emu

Then I'm gonna get me a Teletubby
I'm gonna drive down to Teletubbyland in a van
With a blunderbuss full of All-Bran
And when I come back
I'll have Po strapped to the bonnet
And that bastard handbag still entangled in the wheel of my van
I'm gonna get me a fucking Teletubby

Then I'm gonna get me a Basil Brush
I'm gonna get that aristocratic bushy-tailed bastard in my sights
And then shotgun blast him into next week's *Radio Times*
BOOM BOOM!

Then I'll chop off his hind legs and his tail
I'll keep them
Then I'll throw his bloody carcass back
For his vermin children to feed on
I'm gonna get me a fucking Basil Brush

I don't want no Roland Rat
The disease-ridden glove puppet vermin rat bastard
I want an Ermintrude
Leather jacket and pink suede shoes
You can tell Bernie Clifton and that fucking ostrich of his
You can run
But you can't hide
Barney the dinosaur is extinct
Because I fucking killed him

WE'RE ALL GOING ON A BUNGLE HUNT!

DEAD WOMBLE DISPOSEL
PACKED IN A LEAD VAT (MINIMUM 2F 17LT) OF SALT,
AN ADULT WOMBLE CORPSE SHOULD FULLY BREAK DOWN AND
CORODE, LEAVING ONLY HAIR AND NOSE, IN LESS THAN
6/7 MONTHS

3 FEET DEEP AND SINKING

'3 Feet Deep and Sinking' was the last poem me and Robert performed together, at our final gig in 2007 at The Latitude Festival – the only time we were allowed to support John Cooper Clarke. On hearing that Thick Richard were not performing anymore, Johnny said, "That's what David Bowie said, Thick Richard will be back." I suppose he was right about Thick Richard but he was wrong about Bowie.

Bringing home the bacon is easy for some
Easier said than it is to be done
Well I may as well become a vegetarian
Coz when it comes to bacon, man, I ain't got none
What do you do when you can't afford shoes
Do you keep picking fights that you know you're going to lose?
Well if you've got a party and you want it to be ruined
Call my number and we'll come round and do it
Coz you shouldn't keep quiet when something's not right
And my life feels like a fucking riot
And most of the time
Most of my mind
Is thinking about things that I don't even like
I don't get it
How are you supposed to get with it
When you don't even know where you stand
Because every three weeks something else goes out of fashion
And you end up right back where you fucking began
Who the fuck did I think I was kidding
What a way to make a living
I'm in trouble brother
Pass me that shovel
I'm 3 feet deep and sinking

All the kids on the street point their fingers at me
But one of these days they're going to know how I feel
Marching around like the fashion police

47

Who the fuck dragged you up and made you king
Coz I know that no amount of bellyaching
Is ever going to change the world
Nobody loves us
Everybody hates us
I think I'll go and eat worms
Well I stamp my little feet when I get cross
I stamp them so hard the ground starts to turn soft
And then I wonder why I've started sinking
As I disappear into the quicksand
Who the fuck did I think I was kidding
I'm in trouble brother
Pass me that shovel
I'm 3 feet deep and sinking

And don't go listening to the journalists
Because they can't tell you how deep shit is
And standing onstage saying what Murdoch thinks
Isn't any of my fucking business
Because I've died onstage
More times than a cat's got lives
But I keep getting brought back to life
Man, it's no fucking wonder that I'm tired all the time
Yeah thanks a bunch
You've been a lovely audience
Turning your faces away like my breath stinks
You're all too busy scratching your pants
To even think about clapping your hands
And I know
It sounds like I'm having a moan
I've given up before I've even began
But if you've ever wondered how deep shit goes
Stick around coz I'm about to find out
What the fuck must I have been thinking
What a way to earn a living
I'm in trouble

Pass me that shovel
3 feet deep and sinking

So I'm going to turn my hand
Into the shape of a gun
Shoot you down
Then I'm going to turn my fist
Into the shape of a spade
Dig you a makeshift grave
Make-do funeral for you, you fool
You thought it was a game
Gambled and lost
But at what cost
I'll bite your nose off to spite your face
And drink to the death of Thick Richard
Drink a little too much and end up in a fight
Time to say goodnight Bob
"Goodnight Bob"
Thank you very much
Goodnight

49

Book Two

Thick Richard

THE SUN HAS GOT ITS HOOD UP

I was sitting in the café on The Piccadilly Approach
Watching the commuting drones coming and going
Talking to some homeless bloke with a broken nose
As I slowly arranged my fried breakfast
Into the shape of a sad face
I had a sorry looking sausage for a mouth
Burnt back bacon rashers like *Reservoir Dog* ears
Busted tomato like a sad clown's nose
And baked bean Art Garfunkel hair
This was a snide café though
They'd only given me one fried egg
But I used a triangular hash brown as an eye patch
Which made the plate look uncannily like pop cyclops Gabrielle
Dreams can come true I thought
As I pierced her one good eye with my fork
And I watched her undercooked yellow tears slowly merge
With the grease on her cheeks
Eventually I told the homeless bloke to leave me alone
I left the café without paying
And I made my way to a windowless shoebox size estate pub
Called The Junky's Arms
And there I ordered myself a marriage-wrecking beverage
called The Harpurhey Headbanger
Consists of two parts High Commissioner Whisky, one part
     Cillit Bang and four fingers of distilled Mancunian rain
     water, it's served in a cracked glass ashtray, you're supposed
     to down it in one as the barman smashes you across the
     fucking mouth with it

After my refreshments I was violently escorted
To the car park area where I sat on the wall for a while
Mopping the blood off my face with a dock leaf
And watching a pigeon tying to eat a cigarette end
And it was about this time that winter came to a stop
And the snowdrops melted back into everyday raindrops
The sun has got its hood up
Hip hip hooray
Its curfew starts at seven
It goes in, it's not allowed back out again
Night fell
And put in a compensation claim
And the shadow of the planet cast across the land
Like the ominous shadow of Nosferatu's hand
So I thought I'd better go home
Before someone else tried to beat me up
The bus on the way home smelt as though someone
Had shat themselves
But then looking at the convict cast of passengers
I figured it was probably the driver
At one stop a young man got on
And made a point of sitting on the back seat
And there he proceeded to play terrible tinny music
On a tiny plastic phone
That sounded like some nightmarish fairground
From the early '90s dance era
And to make matters worse he started trying to rap along to it
In that self-conscious style
That sounds like he's being forced to do it against his own will
Eventually it became too much
I turned to him and said...

"Excuse me mate, sorry to interrupt you mid-flow, but I couldn't help but overhear those bars you were just spitting. I actually work as a talent scout for Sony Records and I was just wondering... erm... Could you shut the fuck up! It's just I'm trying to read *The Metro* here and I can't hear myself fucking think!"
And as the young man stabbed me repeatedly in the stomach
My mind wandered back about 20 years ago or so
To when Jarvis sang about
The mis-shapes, the mistakes and the misfits
He promised me a revolution
Where the geeks would inherit the streets
But not by using weapons of muscles
But good manners and minds
...Well it's just one of those things you never get around to doing
I suppose
And as I arrived home that evening
Profusely losing blood
I locked my door behind me
I bolted my windows
I closed my curtains
And my awareness of the inevitable approaching apocalypse
Peaked.

Someone gave an anonymous tip
And a policeman raided my house
He must have been a part-time ventriloquist
Because he kept putting words in my mouth
Nobody shouts anymore
Nobody shouts
You want to be heard
But you don't want to stand out
You want to stand up
But you're afraid to be put down
So nobody shouts anymore
Nobody shouts
What if Rosa Parks just put her iPod on
And shuffled off to the back of the bus?
What if Malcolm X, the Suffragettes and Gandhi
Were all too busy playing Candy Crush?
We don't want to cause a fuss
The last time I spoke out I got punched
And if it looks like you care
You just look like a cunt
So we all just

Nobody shouts anymore
Nobody shouts
You look like a man
But you sound like a mouse
And so we all walk around
With a little black cloud
And nobody shouts
And if they want you to skim over the details
They just make the information boring to read
So we just scroll onto the next newsfeed
"Which political puppet do you be?"
I got Trump
Because I've got about as much clout
As an injured puppy with his teeth pulled out
And if you don't want to die with your hand over your mouth
Then you need to stand up and start shouting about it
Make a banner
That no one will read
Make a stencil
That nobody's going to see
Because you sprayed it on the wall
Of some Northern Quarter hipster street
Where graffiti's been permitted by the police
So what's the fucking point!
Nobody shouts
Nobody shouts
And I'm just a hypocrite
With a big mouth
Because all I did was write a poem about
How nobody shouts anymore
Nobody shhhhhhhhhhhhhhhhhhhhh

BUBBLEGUM PUNK

Bubblegum punk
Bubblegum punk
Plastic plasticine
Fucking rubber punk
Remember that party when we all got drunk
We all started arguing and we all threw up
And then we all started crying when the cops turned up
Oh my god man we're so punk
Your dad's eyeliner all around your eyes
Dressed in an ironic shirt and tie
What possessed you to leave the house
With a haircut that even you're embarrassed about
And you wonder why you keep getting mugged
People keep picking on the bubblegum punk
Imagine being hooked on heroin living in a squat
You never thought people really lived like that
But you don't have to put up with all that shit
Coz you buy your jeans ready ripped
You dick!
I don't own any clothes without holes
I hardly own any clothes that aren't stolen
So put on your Ramones t-shirt
And walk around like you've started a movement
Listen to *Never Mind the Bollocks* if you want
But don't go thinking you just kicked the whole thing off
And don't pretend you don't like Avril Lavigne
Buy all your CDs from HMV
You got a Blink 182 tattoo
You got the piss taken out of you
And you got it removed
Just say no to drugs kids
Don't drink beer and smoke cigs kids
Don't have sex till you're 36 kids

Don't make the same mistakes your parents did
Don't think your shit don't stink kids
Be a bubblegum punk and listen to Pink
And if you want some bad advice
Take my advice
And just do what the fuck you like
If you drink it through a straw you get twice as drunk
You can't get pregnant if you fuck standing up
So keep your feet on the ground
And your head in the clouds
Go wild and don't forget you're allowed
Rave on it's a crazy feeling
Rave on this song has no meaning
I've decided to dance until I die
Fry my mind, drink like suicide
Kill my brain, kill my brain
Get reincarnated and then do it all again
Coz I just keep on piling on
I just keep on piling on
And then just when you think I'm done
I just keep on piling on

So put The Buzzcocks on and we'll all get drunk
Oh fuck
Who invited the bubblegum punk?

SPORTY SPICE

PAULS MUM IS WELL FIT

I ♥ FARTS

ADAM HILL IS GAY

Mr.TICKEL

THE RESION WHY PRE PUBESANT CHILDREN ARN'T ALLOWED TATTOOS.

LIVING WITH THE WALKING DEAD

Every morning when I awake
I see Peter Cushing's face
Hammering a wooden stake into my heart

And then I rise up from the bed
Like the waking of the dead
With a head full of bad dreams, dirt and worms
I tie my tie like a noose
And then before the big commute
I shoot a shot of coffee in my arm
But this energy is fake
Just like the smile on my face
When you ask me how I'm doing
And I tell you I'm ok
Living with the walking dead
Soul-sucking mother-fucking zombies
Left right and centre
When Bruce Campbell is your only friend left
You'd better get used to living with the walking dead
It's hard to tell when you're pushing through the crowds
Which ones are still with us
And which ones we're now living without
But if you look into their eyes you can see
The black hole vacuum where their lives used to live
Awkward walk
Bit wobbly on their feet
They look almost human as they stumble down the street
They have walked lucidly
From George Romero's worst dreams
And now they're pushing on the pull-door
Of the shopping precinct
Because they're easily confused

They don't like thinking
They like shiny colours and bright things
Easily susceptible to advertisements
That's why zombie mums go to Iceland
But it's not the telly's fault
Apathy's to blame
That's what crushes your heart and zombifies your brain
The rot of society should not be ignored
Or else it's only a matter of time until we join them
And I suppose if you think about it Jesus was the original
    zombie wasn't he? Eat my body, drink my blood. Only
    joking folks, that bit's made up!
And that moronic way they try to talk
"Richard, why are you three and a half hours late for work? I
    have to push my way through a coffin door and then
    crawl up through six feet of topsoil, and I manage to get
    into work on time."
Yeah but the difference between you and I is I'm still alive
The bags under your eyes are there coz your soul died
How did I come to be taking orders
From a walking talking re-animated corpse
Of course I never say this
I just fantasise about the day I get to take your head clean off
With a spade
Or drive an armoured van through your house
Crushing your zombified wife and child
Knock you to the ground
Stand on your chest
Press a loaded shotgun to your pulseless neck and say
"This one's for my mate Stuart, who got a job in telesales and
    ended up like one of you fuckers. He said the job was
    only temporary until he found a better one and then he
    went to work in the suit that he was buried in. The look
    on his face as the boss took him to lunch, the soft pop of

his stomach and the smell of his tumbling guts – well, you
won't take *me* alive you soul-sucking flesh-munching cunts,
I'd sooner fall headlong into sweet oblivion"
And then twenty thousand zombies
Come a-bursting through the door
Hungry for an eye-gouging orgy of gore
The future hates me
And it will eat me alive
Infect me with the virus
And turn me on their side
And as the room floods with the walking dead
I turn the gun to my own head
Roll credits
The End

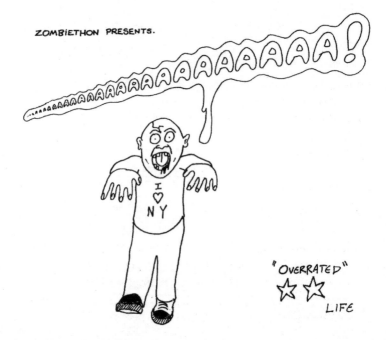

"BUY THE TICKET, TAKE THE RIDE"

You bring the pills, I'll supply the cider
Call work and tell them that my grandad's died
Because I've bought a ticket and I'm taking the ride
We hitched a lift off a friend of a friend
We all got pissed while we pitched the tent
We didn't realise that we weren't in the campsite
Until a horse stepped on my friend's neck
Woke up in a puddle of urine and sweat
At four in the morning in a collapsed tent
The bands haven't even started playing yet
We're already hungover and one of us is dead
Intent on getting out of our minds
As intense as the uncontrolled fire
Yeah that's right
It's festival time
You buy the ticket you take the ride
I woke up buzzing like a neon light
Drank a huge wobbly bottle of White Lightning cider
A Marlboro Light
An outside shite
A packet of Wotsits
And a baby wipe
I dropped a gob full of rancid acid
Fell backwards into my mind
Spent the evening with the St. John's ambulance driver
Stroking my hair reminding me everything's going to be fine
I took a sip of what I thought was water
Span off the face of the Earth
And when I came to about four hours later
I was flat on my back in a yurt
I don't know how I managed to get so drunk
When I can't even afford to eat

Because I've spent all of my money on a bamboo hammock
That I'm too fucking wired to sleep in
And I'm too tired to move an inch
Walking two miles to take a shit in a ditch
Takes the piss
Mate, I don't want to borrow your shovel
I want a door with a lock
And a fucking sink
I gave myself the heebie-jeebies
With some weird time-travelling weed
Watching the bloke out of The Bee Gees
Thinking *Christ where am I*
Nineteen seventy-fucking-three?
And don't mention the weather
It won't be getting any better
We are up to our knees in tears
From the bankrupt crowds of thousands
Who've spent almost a grand to be here
The rain pours down like a pissy sheet
The ground turns to treacle beneath your feet
I'd give a testicle for a seat
The thunderous booming laugh from the sky
As the main stage carries away on a mudslide
Rhianna's umbrella couldn't hold back the tide
She's bought the ticket now she's taking the ride
The Scousers in the tent next door
Went looking for a fight
But despite not being able to play the bongos
They still played the bongos all fucking night
Threw up my guts
Hugging a stomach pump
In the gutter of a country road
If I hadn't been completely covered in slugs
I'd have probably died of exposure

My head's no longer attached to my shoulders
Flails round like a lasso
Like that dead fella who's been going round on the waltzers
Since Saturday afternoon DON'T TOUCH HIM!
I passed out by the dance tent
And got carried away by ants
I had to jettison my pants
Behind a burger van
(Don't ask!)
Something something something... ... ...

TO BE HONEST I CANT REMEMBER
THE END OF THIS POEM. THERE WERE
ANOTHER 4 OR 5 VERSES BUT GOD
KNOWS WHAT THEY WERE. THERE
GONE NOW. BUT I THINK ITS QUITE
FITTING THAT THIS IS A POEM ABOUT
MUSIC FESTIVALS + THAT I CAN ONLY
REMEMBER THE FIRST HALF OF IT.

A SHORT POEM ABOUT FUCKING

The pinch
The squeal
The smack
The scream
The slap
The tickle
The laugh
The plea
The bump
The thump
The naked lunch
The over-emotional pump of the blood
The rough
The tumble
The grapple
The thrust
The rush
The muscle
The pull
The push
The grasp
The clasp
The panting gasp
The frantic ask for faster
The stretch
The tremble
The shudder
The fit
The spasm of passion
The bite of the lip
The frenzied rush
The push
The gush
The quiver
The shiver
The flutter
The flush
The fall
The huddle
The wallow
The roll
The hold
The fold
The envelop

GOD HATES STOCKPORT

If Salford is Manchester's tougher cousin then Stockport is Manchester's boss-eyed smelly cousin that keeps trying to kiss us. I lived there as a teenager and this is all they deserve. I've written some stuff that's got me into trouble before but nothing has earned me more enemies and agro than 'God Hates Stockport'. First time I performed it a man in the audience attacked me after the show. I found out later that he wasn't even from Stockport, he was from Liverpool. Which shows just how offensive this poem is – it can still upset people who live 40 miles away.

Seven miles south of Manchester
There lies a godforsaken land
That even the good Lord himself
Has condemned with his own hand
Some people think it's a fabled place
And don't believe it's real
But I've seen it with my own eyes
And lived to tell the tale
You see
Before Darwin
Before apes and chimps
And original sin
Before God created the Heavens and the Earth
He built Stockport to see if it was worth it
But God's trial run didn't go to plan
Adam ended up more mammal than man
And from that day forth
The land's been cursed
Because God was so furious
And that's the reason why my friends
God hates Stockport
Oh yes
God hates Stockport

He hates their kind and everything they stand for
There's fuck all there except a fancy dress shop
A hat museum and a viaduct
That happens to be the largest brick construction in Europe
Can anybody think of anything more boring!
Even the driver on the 192
Doesn't want to go there so she just drives straight through
Up on past Denton to Hyde
From the eleven-fingered beady-eyed baby-eaters of Reddish
God hates Stockport
These people aren't like you and I
They're terrified of outsiders
A black man tried to run for mayor
They stuck him in a wicker man and set it on fire
These people aren't like you and me
They still eat their offspring
They killed a girl because she was born ginger
I can't join the library coz I've only got ten fingers
And if you're out after dark you'd better run on home
These roads are owned by the 14 year olds
Sitting on the corner of the park on his own
Smoking a no-roach papery roll
Venereal disease
He smells of yeast
He spits when he speaks because he's got no teeth
An amphetamine abscess on the back of his knee
The kid's only 14 and he's wanted by the police
Kid, you're such an inbred
Your mother is your brother and your sister is your dad
If they're the kind of games you play
Then it's no fucking wonder that you all look the same
But with a pure bloodline like these
Inbreeding produces a special species
The hunchback of Cheadle Hulme

Who's allergic to sunlight
And the three-eyed girl from Stepping Hill
Who can predict how you're going to die
Smelly people!
And you might say "Oh don't be like that
My gran's from Stockport and she's not bad"
Bollocks!
She's an arsehole
So fuck her
Fuck you
And fuck everything you stand for

God hates Stockport

NEW VOODOO FUNERAL BLUES

*In 1929 notorious gambler and pimp Jesse Williams was shot by the
police. His friend, legendary Blues man Blind Willie McTell, helped
him back home to his death bed. McTell sat at his bedside for the three
weeks it took Jesse to die and during this time he dictated to him the
details he wished for his funeral, including a deck of cards for his
tombstone, the high sheriff playing blackjack leading the parade and a
gathering of prostitutes from around the country at his graveside. He
told him to make a song of his requests which is called 'The Dying
Crapshooter's Blues' and McTell sang it as they buried him. Apparently,
apart from a few of the prostitutes who were uncontactable, Jesse
Williams got everything he asked for at his funeral. This poem is a re-
writing of that song and is about how I would like to be disposed of
once I am dead.*

Blind Willie McTell and Jesse Williams wrote this song
Sincerely
I don't care what you do with me when I'm gone
Really
Boil or fry me
I don't mind
Bawling and crying's just a waste of time
Wrap me up in a rug and chuck me down a mine
I got the new voodoo funeral blues
I got the new voodoo what you won't dare do
The new voodoo funeral blues
Because you wouldn't put a garnish on a chicken carcass
New voodoo funeral blues
There is a service here required to be met
A disrespect for the dead
I want to be thrown from a speeding car and just left
The new voodoo funeral blues
I want a gang of disinterested teenage rapscallions
To throw my remains in a sack
I want nine of us driving down to the rubbish tip, buddy

But only eight of us coming back
At six o'clock I want a man and his dog
To find me and turn a blind eye
I want a policeman whistling inconspicuously
As he strolls by
I want a bunch of lilies tied to the bus stop
Where I was last seen alive
And any trace of my personal past
Either forgotten or lost in a fire
And when they roll me out on that slab
I want them to stifle a laugh
I want my DNA to turn up in a Findus lasagne
Béchamel sauce
Pasta sheets
My toenail stuck in your fucking teeth
May I be excused from the table please
I've got the new voodoo funeral blues
I don't want my face on no stamp
Stick my picture on a cigarette pack
Burn me up good like an oily rag
And flick my ash into a Special Brew can
I want a chest freezer for my coffin
And cling film for my burial clothes
I want you to taxider-*me* into a wanking pose
I don't want to be sedated
Not sure whether I'm alive or dead?
Just hide me under Shannon Matthews' bed
I've got the new voodoo funeral blues

DEAR ROWNTREES

I BOUGHT A BAG OF YOUR RANDOMS LAST FRIDAY FROM THE SHOP ON THE CORNER. THE BAG CONTAINED A TOTAL OF 13 SWEETIES, THE FIRST 3 OF THESE WERE UNMEMORABLE BUT NOT UNPLESANT. HOWEVER, I TOOK THE LAST 10 RANDOMS OUT OF THE BAG IN THE FOLLOWING ORDER.

SHUTTLE COCK
CRICKET BAT
FOOTBALL
FOOT
SOCK
SHOE
FOOTBALL (AGAIN!)
WHISTLE
TRUMPET
GIRAFF

WHIT THE EXEPTION OF GIRAFF THIS CAN IN NO WAY BE CONSIDERD A RANDOM LIST AS EACH SWEET IS ODVIOUSLY ASSOCIATED WITH THE ONE PRESEADING IT + THE ONE FOLLOWING IT. THIS IS THE 19TH DRAFT OF THIS LETTER THAT IVE WRITTEN + I AM STILL AT A LOSS FOR WORDS TO CONVEY THE DISAPOINTMENT I FELT AT THE SHEER RANDOMLESSNESS I WAS CONFRONTED WITH INSIDE THAT BAG OF SWEETS + THE BETTRALE THAT STILL ACHES WITHIN ME FROM SUCH A MISSLEADING PRODUCT NAME.

I STRONGLY URGE YOU TO LAY OFF YOUR ENTIRE STAFF ON THE GROUNDS OF FAILING TO GRASP THE CONCEPT OF RANDOMNESS SO MISRIBLY, FAILING THAT MAY I SUGGEST YOU CHANGE THE NAME 'RANDOMS' TO THE NAME 'RELIVANCES' TO PREVENT ANY MORE OF YOUR CUSTOMERS HAVING TO SUFFER THE SAME ORDEAL I DID.

TO ADD TO THE MONOTONY OF YOUR PREDICTABLE TREAT ALL OF THESE SWEETS WERE GREAN,

WITH THE EXEPTION OF GIRAFF. ADMITEDLY IT IS UNLIKELY GETTING 10 CONSECUTIVE GREEN SWEETS IN ONE PACK, PREHAPS DEMONSTRATEING THE RANDOM NATURE

OF CHANCE, HOWERVE GREEN IS BY FAR YOUR MOST UNPLESANT FLAVOR + SO I AM STILL INCLUDING THIS AS PART OF MY ORIGIONAL COMPLAINT.

TRUSTING YOU STILL VALUE YOUR CUSTOMERS OPINION I HAVE HERE INCLUDED A LIST OF RANDOM SHAPES THAT I FOR ONE WOULD LIVE TO SEE INCLUDED IN YOUR SELECTION

VINIGER
HARIBO FRYED EGG
LOZENGE
DAPPYS LIPS
SAND
FISH FINGER CRUSIFIX WITH CRAB CHRIST
RADIO 4
CILLA BLACK[1]

I FEEL IVE OVERSTATED MY POINT NOW. IM ACTUALLY BEGINING TO REGRET WRITEING THIS LETTER TO BE HONEST. I AM VERY LONLEY.

LONLEY
MATT DUFFY
X

(I THOUGHT FROM THE LEVEL OF SARCASM I USED IN THIS LETTER I WAS ODVIOUS ALL I WANTED WAS A FREE BAG OF SWEETS. IF YOUR COMPLAINING TO NESTLE + YOU'VE GOT THE DECENCY NOT TO MENTION ALL THOUSE AFRICAN CHILDREN THEY MURDERD YOU THINK THEY WOULD SHOW THERE APPRECIATION BY DISHING OUT THE SWEETS! BUT NO. ALL THEY SENT ME WAS THIS LETTER. TOSSERS.

---

[1] No disrespect to Cilla! Check the date on the reply – this was written long before Cilla died. And, thinking about it, it would be a lovely tribute to her (especially in orange!).

...tle ...Ltd
YORK YO91 ...

Nestle

Register with Nestlé for the latest
product news & special offers
www.nestle.co.uk

Matthew Duffy
71 Milford Street
Stretford
MANCHESTER
Greater Manchester
M32 8AC

DIRECT LINE: 0800 000030

DATE

DIRECT FAX: 01904 803461

003071812A   27 March 2012

Dear Matthew

Thank you for getting in touch about Rowntrees Randoms.

We are so sorry that your bag of Randoms was a poor selection from the hundreds of different
sweets in the assortment. We produce four different textures and six natural fruit flavours. In total
there are 70 shapes and this creates a potential for 258 random shape and colour combinations.

Randoms contain real fruit juice and have no artificial colours or flavours. Each Randoms bag
should contain a completely different mix from any other, providing a spontaneous and random
experience every time. We hope your next bag will be much more exciting.

Thank you once again for taking the time and trouble to contact us. We hope you will continue to
enjoy our products in the future.

Yours sincerely

Debbie W...
Contact Centre Officer
Consumer Services

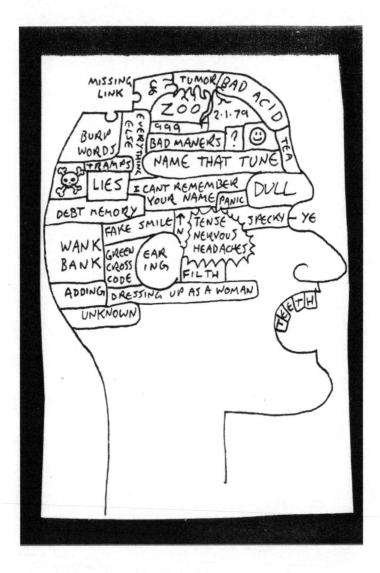

74

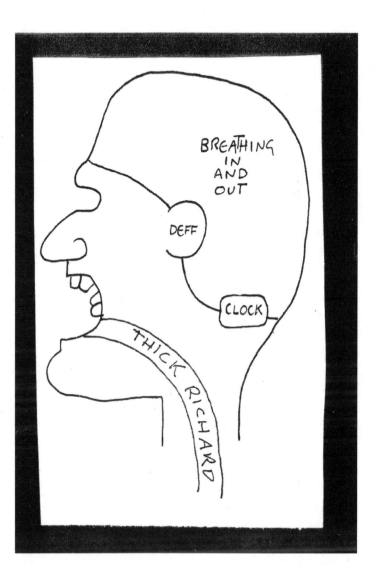

75

IF WOMEN LIKE THEM LIKE MEN LIKE THOSE THEN WHY DON'T WOMEN LIKE ME?

Written to the tune of 'Why Don't Women Like Me' by George Formby.

Last night I went out walking
My intentions were to click
But the sights I saw whilst walking out
They almost made me sick
I saw some stunning woman
Whose boyfriend beggared belief
Some bog-eyed bastard with skin rash
Club foot and missing teeth
Now if women like them like men like those
Then why don't women like me?
What could the attraction be
He looks like an ugly George Formby
If he was a boxer I could understand
But he's just a shelf-stacker down in Matalan
If women like them like men like those
Why don't women like me?
In a club full of arseholes giving me the elbow
In comes Cupid carrying a crossbow
He just shoots the first thing that moves
Clicks his fingers and they form a queue
Jonny Heartless you're so cool
We want to be just like you
He treats 'em mean and he keeps 'em keen
Vera Duckworth's initials on his car keys
The fact he's good looking becomes irrelevant
His flat's a shithole coz his closet's full of skeletons
The ladies love a bastard
Well that's my problem there
Coz I'm just a twat
But if women like them like men like that
Why don't women like me?

I kissed a bloke
I didn't like it
It seemed like a good idea at the time but...
I kissed a bloke
I didn't like it
It tasted like Fray Bentos pie

Well what you make up in charm
You're lacking in looks
You were dealt an unfortunate mug
That even your mother must struggle to love
A face which I wouldn't want to chop wood on
Pigeon chested
Manorexic
Smells a bit like disinfectant
Nothing respectable to begin with
Spectacles bigger than bin lids
Fake watch
White socks
A flatulence problem that happens too often
Intense stare
Nostrils flared
Teeth bared
No hair
Perry Combover Beethoven
Napalm breath
Talk to you over the phone and I can still smell it
It's like someone opening a packet of dry roasted peanuts
And a cat yawning in your face at the same fucking time
Eyes like a lizard
Skin like an amphibian
From a distance looks a bit like Ann Widdecombe
Can't be the money coz he's always skint
Nevertheless the women are all over him
In fact he's trying to beat them off with a shitty stick

Now if women like them like men like it
Why don't women like me?
What could the attraction be?
Paul Daniels hypnotising Debbie McGee
I don't think Colleen Rooney's all that hot
But stood next to Wayne she's a fucking work of art
If women like men like men like those
Why don't women like me?
Black butterfly eyelashes flirt and flutter
On a lily-white heart-shaped face
You fit your body like a leg into a stocking
An untouchable picture of grace
But flowery compliments aside
I think your taste in guys leaves a lot to be desired
In fact you must be out of your beautiful mind
Coz if women like you like men like them
Why don't women like me (*hey hey!*)
Why don't women like me?

BAD PENNY RABBIT

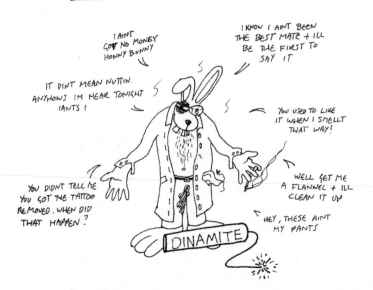

SCUM OF THE EARTH

I was conceived in the recovery position
In the basement of a police station
I was brought up like a ballerina's breakfast
And raised on stolen donations
The doctor cried
The midwife resigned
As I was born to this world
My mother swapped me for a less ugly baby
And she called me the scum of the earth

Scum of the earth
The name that I was baptised as a babe
Lightning struck the steeple of the church
When the priest called out my name
He threw his Bible in the sky
Pulled out a pistol
And shot a hole through it like a bird
And as its feathers came spiralling down to the ground
He christened me the scum of the earth

Scum of the earth
Untrustworthy
Bound to be up to no good
Standing on the outskirts of society
Swigging from a bottle of angel's blood
Peeping over the precipice
Forever the pessimist
Even my blood group is bleeding negative
Counting on your fingers to calculate my worth
And you call me the scum of the earth

Depending on the state
Of mind I'm in when I awake
I might partake in playing nice
And join in with your game
But unemployment's got its benefits
You can't get fired
And I know the system doesn't work
So why the fuck should I?

(To the tune of 'Gold' by Spandau Ballet)

Dole (dole)
Always believe in your soul
You've got nowhere to go
Your unemployable
Always believe in dole

Well I've always got my settee to fall back on [2]
How much is your time worth
When I sign on
I sign the name you gave me
Scum of the earth

And the calendar pages pave the way
Of a 75 year long street
And so I bang my head
Against the factory wall
There ain't nothing to do but drink
There ain't nothing to do
But abuse the booze
And kiss goodbye to the day

OH JESUS NO

It's enough to make a man lose his screws
Man, I just want to get in my grave
Because I'm just a mild-mannered social parasite by day
But after six and a half hours on the apple sauce
An amazing transformation takes place...

Cider-man! Cider-man!
I can't do it but I think I can
Because only a pissed-up superhero
Or a complete fucking idiot
Would try and pick a fight with a police dog
That line didn't scan
There goes the Cider-man

Well I had a most terrible daydream
As I was propping up the end of the bar
My life fragmented into millions of jigsaw pieces
And scattered all over the floor
And franticly on my hands and knees I try picking up the shards
And piecing it back together again
But the picture looked all wrong
I ran to the toilets to throw up
And this scream of unconsciousness spewed from my gut
I staggered back to the bar wiping my face
But the expressions on the people's faces had changed

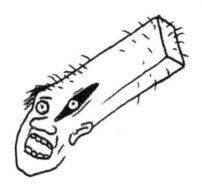

"What's your poison?" the barman asked
I saw terrible visions in the bottom of my glass
I saw the mass replicated definition of freedom
Represented by the slogans printed on the t-shirts
To corrupt the pupil you poison the teachers
I heard the untrustworthy word being preached
By the diehard disciples of Saturday night TV
Who like to make you think life's just a rehearsal
Because it helps to cope with the hurt
That comes with the curse of being a person
A brand new definition of worthlessness
And they plead
And they scream
"Pick me!
We just want to be living the dream!"
Well they obviously don't have the same dreams as me
Unless they want to be chased around a burning house
By Foxy Bingo
Naked!
With a massive erection the size of a prize-winning marrow

But, you know...
Each to their own
And this blinding clarity is like a pencil in my eye
Take your dick out of my ear and stop fucking with my mind!
"What's your poison?" the barman asked
I saw terrible visions in the bottom of my glass
And I screamed at the people to warn them
But they just turned back to their drinks and ignored me
And then the management asked me to leave

NNNNNggHHHNNN!!!!!

So now I'm outside shouting at the traffic on the street
Shaking my fist at the useless moon
Trying to catch the stupid thing with a lasso
Maybe I'm just confused
But I can't seem to see the world the way that I used to
But you've made your mind up
You know all you need to know
You see me coming and you cross the road
Like that chicken in the joke
But your narrow mind is too small to look down on me
Class never has been a straight line
And respect is a two-way street
The land that your cattle are reared on is poisoned
The fruit your trees bare manufactured by man
Your media and art is corrupted by money
And therefore irrelevant to me and my clan
Your wealth is like time
A powerful concept
Which when studied closely doesn't actually exist
What will you do when the people you put down discover
The foundations of your house are so weak they will split
So I'll just leave you to worry about things
Like reputation and worth
But just remember this planet is made out of dirt
When you call me the scum of the earth

AAAAAA AAAAAAAHHHHHHH HHHHHHHHHHHH!

---

[2] Line supplied by Hovis Presley, R.I.P.

Book Three

The Sound of
One Fan Clapping

A MILLION MONKEYS WITH A MILLION TYPE WRITERS WOULD HAVE WRITTEN THIS BOOK IN A MATTER OF MUINETS. IT TOOK ME ALMOST 20 YEARS. FROM STAGE TO PAGE, 20 FUCKING YEARS! (ALMOST) THIS CHAPTER IS THE BEST BITS OF THE SHIT YOU MIGHT HAVE MISSED, ODD JOBS, BITS + BOBS + LESSER KNOWN KEEPERS THAT NO BODY REMEMBERS BUT ME. FUCK KNOWS HOW I REMEMBERD THEM! I DEDICATE THESE PAGES TO THE HUNDREDS OF NAMES IVE SHARED THE STAGES WITH, WAY, WAY TOO MANY NAMES TO NAME, HERES TO THE DAYS OF GETTING PAID IN ALE TO SPEND AGES ON STAGE GETTING WASTED...

THE
SOUND
OF
ONE
FAN
CLAPPING

INVISIBLE ENEMIES

The world you know is under attack
The life you love is under threat
Everything you know is just lies and fairytales
The whole show's run by a bunch of charlatans
The revolution is never going to happen
And there is nothing you can do
You need your broadband too badly
You haven't even got time to chew your food
So how you gonna find time to draw up your plans
How you gonna make your voice heard
Do you really think people are losing sleep
Over just another person in the world
Who the fuck said you could do what you want?
I think you should go back and look at the facts
The man's got what you want
And he told me he ain't gonna give it back
There's no such thing as an accident
Everything's been timed down to a tease
So don't count on my vote suckers
Why should I, what's in it for me?
I'm making a list, a long list
I'm making a list and checking it twice
Of people who truly believe that they have a say
In what goes on in their lives
And don't start dreaming that you've got something to believe in
Coz none of what you know is fact
The only things you know are things that other people told you
And you know you can't believe a word of that
They've got you by the bollocks and they ain't letting go
And so they sent me here tonight to let you know
That the revolution is never going to happen
And there is nothing that you can do

HEY KIDS!

Just a note
To let you know
That we know you know what we know
And we know you don't want us to know it
But it's foolish to think we don't
We know that you know all about
The sordid secret "ins and outs"
Of things only grown-ups should do
We know the internet told you
We know you sometimes laugh out loud
To jokes that you don't get
Coz you don't want to seem naïve
In front of all your friends
We know when you get home
You research what these new words mean
That leads you to seeing things
You know you shouldn't see
We know you only pretend
Not to like the things you did
When you were eight
Coz all your mates say that stuff's just for kids
Did you know all the bigger
Tougher
Much maturer kids
All have bedrooms full of childhood teddy bears
And sentimental gifts
We know the language that you use
When you're just with your friends
We've seen the YouTube video
Your older cousin sent
We know you smoke
And we know you don't know
If you're into girls or blokes
How do we know?

Coz when we were growing up
We didn't know if we were coming or going!
We know you can't wait to grow up
And show off getting drunk
Tell the boss to stuff his job
And eat nothing but sugar
"No one tells me what to do because I'm 21"
It might seem a million miles away
But one day that day will come
There is just one small fact of life
That we know you don't know
A small nugget of wisdom
Only gained from growing older
It might not be what you want to hear
But sometimes the truth hurts
Growing up
Yeah it might suck
But being grown-up is worse!

THE BAD MANNERED MAN

So I decided to take my work back underground
To stop it falling into the wrong hands
I can't show my face around town
Ever since I started hanging around with the wrong crowd
I can count my friends on one hand
On account of all the fights that we've had
So I sat myself down and drew up a plan
I didn't take into account the bad mannered man

The bad mannered man walks into the room
Wearing his skin-tight pin-stripe suit
When the bad mannered man speaks to you
My god you know you've been spoken to
A massive intellect without an ounce of respect
Every girl's available and every man's a threat
Everyone's an enemy and everyone's a pest
When your only life's pursuit is money and sex

Hey Eve who's that man
Standing in your garden with an apple in his hand?
Who's that snake there with the fake tan?
Well don't look now but it's the bad mannered man
The bad mannered man came round to my house
He didn't say much just lay on my couch and slept
Then four days later he left
A whole load of questions unanswered

Who is that bad mannered man?
What does he want and where does he come from?
I heard he fights dirty, heard he causes harm
I heard he turned talking hard into a form of art
I don't think he likes you all that much
The way he slapped your face with that black leather glove
And then asked you to step outside the room
Said there's some two-fisted business to tend to

Your girl left you and you never felt so bad
You thought you had a plan about winning her back
But when you saw her again she was flapping like a flag
She couldn't stop thinking about that bad mannered man
No one's ever spoken to her like that
With such little respect
Smoked all her cigarettes
Slept in her bed
And just got up and left
Oh yeah but admit it girl
You loved every minute of it

Cast your mind back to when you were young
And what your father told you when you left home
He said don't trust a man
Who doesn't like Dylan
And don't shake hands with the bad mannered man
And did you listen
No you didn't
And now you're wondering how
He took your girl without so much as a please
Or a thank you
Pull yourself together lad
You're flapping like a flag
You just can't stop thinking about that bad mannered man

A PRAYER FOR THE WORKING—CLASS
CAPITALIST BASTARD

Written to the tune of 'Down in the Ground Where the Dead Men Go'
by The Pogues.

Oh Lord won't you buy me a Mercedes Benz
Oh Lord won't you help me pay the rent
I really need the new West Brom away kit
I really need my living room floor laminated
I can't be bothered getting a job
So instead I've started bothering God
My Bible is the Argos catalogue
Because I don't know the difference between need and want
I'm living in a material world
Every so often I go to church
I get down and I thank the Lord
For keeping the wolf away from my door
Oh Jesus
Please can you arrange
For all of my debts to be in one place
Just one easy monthly payment
Because I'm up to my apricots in CCJs
There's a plasma screen TV I've seen
Carries a seven-year guarantee
Christ I'm down on my bended knees
Won't you make my dreams a reality please
Oh Jesus
I've seen this red leather couch
I really don't think I can live without
Just give me those thirty pieces of silver
And I swear on your father I'll become a believer
I'm a believer!
I believe!!
My favourite seventh sin is greed
And you can take it with you
Coz I'm riding in Hades

Inside a Mercedes Benz
And I've been told
For a handful of gold
You can buy yourself a brand new soul

Down in the ground where the dead men go
I'm going down in the ground where the dead men go

So... TELL me about hell!

THUMBPRINT

Leopard skin
Smoke ring
Handcuff
Thumbprint
Lipstick
Mattress
Chipped nail varnish
Dress in drag
Wear a mask
Union Jack crotchless pants
Have you seen the size of that bouncer
Well don't touch unless you know how to
Keyhole
Peepshow
Take a look
Some guy gets busy with a bucket and a mop
Tooth sucking pimp in a pussy fur coat
Teenage woman in her birthday suit
Stick it
Where it
Doesn't fit
Kiss with the lips that you've never kissed with
The names have been changed to protect the innocent
Leopard skin
Smoke ring
Handcuff
Thumbprint

THE CLOCK TICKED BACKWARDS

Written to the tune of 'The Room Got Heavy' by Yo LaTengo.

Well
The night was dark
Like the Masonic arts
It was hot and claustrophobic
Like a stolen car
The music was intense
Like a time bomb clicking
Heavy and monotonous
Like prison cell bricks
The building was decrepit and fucked
And it looked
Like a concrete tramp struggling to stand up
It was the ideal space for an all-night rave
You could feel it pulsate from a mile away
Everybody looks like a bouncer
Everybody looks like they know what's about to go down
So I tried not to look too frightened
I just slipped into the crowd
Tried not to stand out
Here, why don't you take one of these?
Take two for a really deep sleep
Take three if you want to get fucked
But don't take four or you won't wake up
Suddenly the atmosphere it kicks in
The clock ticked backwards
The room did a backspin
Someone pulled the plug on the tension
Made the hairs on the back of my neck
Stand up and start paying attention
The dancefloor is some gorgeous war
We move like we're dancing underwater

The clock ticked backwards and my bubble of thought
Burst with the force of a mother-fucking juggernaut
Somebody's fucked with my flux capacitor
The night moves forwards but the clock ticks backwards
In a room full of strangers
Fucking telepathically
My heartbeat has a happy panic attack
And then my blood starts pumping like a tubeway train
Through a subterranean network of electric veins
My skeleton glows through my skin like an x-ray
The clock ticked backwards
The night began again
The alcohol flowed
The cigarettes smoked
The clock ticked backwards but the night kept going
Venus in Adidas dances too fast
As the Halloween patterns creep from out of the cracks
Then the momentum staggered
The sun hits the sky
So we ran for the shadows and we hid like vampires
There goes another night locked in the past
I remember everything
The clock ticked backwards

ISSUE
1

R·R·P
£4
N·U·S
£5

THICK RICHARD

THE
WASTE
PAPPER
UPDATES

TYSON TATTOO PRESS

WEDNESDAY
7.00 AM
WOKE UP EARLY THIS MORNING, I WAS VERY
PLEASED TO DISCOVER I CAN SUCK MYSELF
OFF, LIKE PRINCE DOSE. IVE BEEN TRYING
TO DO IT FOR YEARS + NOW I CAN!!
WHAT A SPLENDID WAY TO START THE DAY.
SMIELY FACE! ☺

10.45 AM
IGNORE MY LAST UPDATE, I CANT SUCK
MY OWN COCK. I WAS JUST STILL
ASLEEP + DREAMING I COULD. VERY
REALISTIC! TURNS OUT ID JUST FELL
OUT OF BED + GOT ME SELF WEDGED
BENT DOUBBLE BETWEEN THE
MATTRES + THE WARDROBE AGAIN.
DISAPOINTED! ☹

11.00 AM

WELL, TODAYS THE DAY! I HAVE AN
APONTMENT BOOKED AT THE TATTOO PARLOR
TO HAVE A PORTRAITE OF MY GIRLFRIENDS
FACE TATTOOED ONTO MY CHEST BETTWEEN
MY NIPPLES + NAVEL AS A SYMBOL OF
MY UNDIEING LOVE. NOT TOLD HER YET,
ITS A SUPRISE, SO OBVIOUSLY I COULDNT ASK
HER FOR A PHOTO. SO AFTER RUMAGING
THROUGH HER STUFF YESTERDAY THE ONLY
ONE I COULD FIND WAS OF HER SCREMING
+ CRYING ON THE OBLIVION AT ALTON
TOWERS. WELL, ITS JUST GOING TO
HAVE TO DO, IM SUURE SHELL LOVE
IT. JUST GOING TO SHAVE MY TORSO
NOW + THEN NIP OUT TO GET SOME
BREAKFAST BEFOR I SET OFF.
ILL KEEP YOU POSTED.

11·37 AM

JUST NIPPED OUT TO GET SOME BREAKFAST
+ FOUND MY NEIGHBOURS FLAT HAS BEEN
TURNED INTO A TESCO METRO OVER NIGHT.
CONVENIENT! THE NEWSPAPER HEADLINES AT
THE CIGGY COUNTER SAID THAT WALLACE
OFF OF WALLACE + GROMIT IS THE LATEST
CELLEBRITY TO BE CAUGHT UP IN THE RECENT
PEDOPHILE SCANDAL. I WAS PRETTY SHOKED AT
FIRST, BUT, IF YOU THINK ABOUT IT, IT WAS
QUITE ODVIOUS. ANYWAY, TESCO WERE FLOGGING
ALL THERE WALLACE + GROMIT RELATED
~~~~ MERCHEDICE FOR NEXT TO NOUT, PROBABLY
AFRAID PEOPLE MIGHT ASSOCIATE THE NAME
TESCO WITH THE PUPPY DOG PEDELING PLASTACINE
PEDO. I SNAPED UP 26 SHAUN THE SHEEP
BIRTHDAY CAKES FOR 8 QUID. THAT SHOULD
KEEP ME GOING FOR THE REST OF
THE WEEK.
            NOM NOM

12:50 AM

- I REALLY NEED TO GET A DOCTORS APPOINTMENT BOOK + GET HIM TO SORT MY ARSE OUT. + IM NOT ANTISIPATEING ANY GOOD NEWS.

- IVE JUST EATEN 3 BIRTHDAY CAKES + HAD TO TAKE A KAK AFTER + NOW ITS STARTED COMING OUT LIKE SAND, JUST A SLOW TRICKLE, LIKE AN EGG TIMER, COLO TO THE TOUCH + IT HURTS.

- COLD RED DUST ISNT ON THE BRISTOL STOOL CHART. WHATS WRONG WITH ME ? IT TOOK AGES TO CLEAN UP + NOW MY ARSE FEELS LIKE AN UNFOLDED MAP THAT I CAN'T PUT AWAY.

IM OFF TO GET THE BUS.

(⌣_⌣)

1·38 PM

JESUS! YOU WONT BELIVE WHAT
JUST HAPPEND TO ME!! I WAS SAT
THERE, ON THE DOWNSTAIRS OF THE BUS
ON ME WAY TO THE TATTOO PARLOR
TO GET A FULL SIZE PORTRAITE OF
MY GIRLFRIENDS FACE PERMINENTLY
ECHED INTO MY CHEST +, I THINK,
I DIED. IM PRETTY SHURE THATS WHAT
HAPPEND, I THINK. I WENT ALL DIZZY
+ EVERYTHING WENT BLACK + FOGGY
+ I WENT ALL DEAD. I JUST SUDENLY
DIED, ANYHOW I ALWAYS CARRY MY
DONNAS CARD ON ME AND, AS LUCK
WOULD HAVE IT, A GAS EXPLOSION ON
THE OTHER SIDE OF TOWN LEFT THIS BLOKE
IN NEED OF SKIN, BONES, BLOOD, A
BRAIN, EYES, HAIR, A HEART, BASICLY
HE INHERETED ME. I DONATED MY
ENTIRE SELF + IT SEAMS IVE GOT A
SECOND CHANCE. THE WEIRD THING IS
I NOW HAVE TO SHARE THE INSIDE OF
MY HEAD WITH A 49 YEAR OLD GAS

MAN CALLED RUSSLE WHO IS NOW THE LIFE
FORCE TO MY SECOND HAND MACHINE. HE
SEAMS LIKE A NICE BLOKE. HE'S A
BIT LIKE ONE OF MY IMAGINARY FRIENDS,
EXEPT, HE'S **REAL!** I DON'T REMEMBER
~~THE HOSPITAL OR THE OPERATION, BUT
THEN AGAIN, I WAS DEAD.~~ RUSSLE TOLD
ME ALL ABOUT IT, SOUNDED HORIBLE. I
CANT RECALL A THING. I JUST WOKE
UP ON THE BUS, WITH RUSS, + THE
BUS DRIVER SHOUTING AT ME TO GET OFF
THE BUS. ANYWAY. IM HERE NOW TO
GET MY TATTOO.

CALL PHILL
08457 90
90

3.55 PM. UNBELIVABLE! ID JUST GOT TO THE TATTOOISTS
TO GET MY TATTOO DONE WHEN MY GIRLFREND SENT ME A
MESSAGE SAYING SHE DOSNT WANT TO SEE ME AGAIN + IF I GO
ANYWHERE NEAR HER ILL HAVE TO GO BACK TO PRISION APARENTLY
SHES 'AFFRAID OF ME' + SHE WANTS ME TO STOP CALLING HER MY
GIRLFRIEND, I MEAN, WHAT DOSE SHE EXPECT ME TO CALL HER
IF SHE WON'T TELL ME WHAT HER REAL NAME IS THE
STUPID BITCH! RUSS SAID I SHOULD STILL GET THE
TATTOO DONE BUT I SHOULD GET IT DONE UPSIDE DOWN, THAT
WAY I CAN STILL LOOK AT HER WHEN IM WANKIN, SHE'LL
ALWAYS LOOK YOUNG + SHE WON'T DO THAT NERVOUS FLINCHY
BLINKING FACE WHEN I SMAFF OVER HER. RUSS IS DEAD
CLEVER. HES GOT LOADS OF GOOD IDEAS. I HAVE TO GO
BACK TOMOROW TO GET HER COLORED IN

THUMBS UP!

4.15 PM   ME + RUSSLE TOOK A WALK
ROUND THE CANNALS + ATE OUR TEA.
FEEL A BIT WOOZY AFTER THE TATTOO
+ THE BANDAGES ARE DEAD ICHY. WE SAT
+ WACHED 2 COUNCIL CLEANERS TRYING TO
FISH A DEAD MERMAID OUT OF THE CANAL
WITH A COUPLE OF BUTTERFLY NETS. THE
SMELL PUT ME RIGHT OF MY BIRTHDAY CAKE
SO I THREW IT IN THE WATER. RUSSLE
TOLD ME ALL ABOUT MYSELF HIMSELF.
HE'S A GENIUS, HE'S SO CLEVER. HE KNOWS
LOADS OF STUFF ABOUT LOADS OF THINGS
IVE NEVER EVEN THOUGHT ABOUT. HE
TOLD ME HOW INCETS ARE ACTUALY TINY
ROBOTS BUILT BY THE ROYAL FAMILY TO
GATHER FOOD FOR THEM + THAT THERES
NO LAW AGAINST BEING NAKED FROM THE
WAIST DOWN, JUST AS LONG AS THE SOALS
OF YOUR FEET ARE COVERD. HE SAID
THAT MY GIRLFRIEND IS JUST PLAYING
HARD TO GET + THAT I SHOULD BE

PERSISTANT, BECAUSE WOMEN LIKE THAT IN
A MAN + HE SAID I SHOULDNT LISTEN TO
OTHER PEOPLE BECAUSE THEY DONT LIKE
ME. HE TOLD ME THAT, IF THE MAN WHO
INVENTED THE WASHING MACHINE HAD
INVENTED THE TELEVISION INSTED, THAT
T·V SCREANS WOULD BE ROUND + THAT
OLD PEOPLE DONT MIND DIEING. I WONDER
IF WALLACE EVER DID IT TO MORPH? OR IS
MORPH OLDER THAN WALLACE? I BET TONY
HEART POKED A HOLE THRU BOTH OF THEM
THE DIRTY BEADY EYED BASTARD. WE BOTH
STARTED TO FEEL SICK. RUSS SAYS WE
NEED SOME FRUIT TO KEEP OUR STRENGTH
UP SO WERE OFF TO THE GREENGROCERS
TO GET SOME POTATOES

AS WE WALKED I TOOK THE BANDAGES
OFF + THREW THEM INTO THE CANAL.

4.55 PM.

- [ ] I GOT INTO A BIT OF A QUARREL AT
- [ ] THE FRUIT + VEG SHOP. I WAS TRYING
- [ ] TO EXPLANE TO THIS OLD FELLA HOW
- [ ] THE VACUME CLEANER HENNRY HOOVER
- [ ] IS THE ORIGIONAL CYBORG, WICH HE
- [ ] FUCKING WELL IS! RUSSLE KNOWS
- [ ] LOADS ABOUT ROBOTS + HE SAYS A
- [ ] CYBORG IS A HUMAN RESEMBLING
- [ ] ANDROID BUILT TO CARRY OUT MENIAL
- [ ] TASKS + IN REAL LIFE HENRY HOOVER
- [ ] IS THE FIRST APLIANCE TO FIT THIS
- [ ] DESCRIPTION, BUT, THIS OLD GEEZER
- [ ] DIDN'T WANT TO SEE MY POINT OF
- [ ] VIEW. HE EVEN AT ONE POINT TRYED
- [ ] TO SLY HIS WAY OUT OF THE DEBATE
- [ ] BY LEAVING THE SHOP, WICH REALY

GOT MY BACK UP. RUSSLE SAID I
SHOULD JOG AFTER HIM + I DID. WHEN
I CAUGHT UP I DELT HIM A SWIFT
RYTHMICAL 5 OR 6 BEATS TO THE
FACE. THIS SENT HIM STUMBELING
BACKWARDS OVER A SMALL BARON OF
SATSUMAS WICH ROLLED ALL OVER THE
ROAD. ONCE I HAD HIM ON THE GROUND I
KNELT OVER HIM + STARTED BRINGING MY
FORHEAD DOWN ONTO HIS FACE AGAIN +
AGAIN + AGAIN UNTILL HE LOOKED
LIKE A PILE OF BUBBELING MINCE
WITH SOME TEETH IN IT + A PAIR OF
BROKEN GLASSES. RUSSLE SAID THE
BUS WAS COMEING + WE HAD TO GO.

5.00 PM
I KNOCKED AN OLD LADY OVER AS WE
RAN FOR THE BUS. RUSSLE STARTED
LAUGHING SO MUCH HE ALMOST
CHOKED ON HIS POTATO + WAS
SICK A BIT. I WAS GOING TO GO
BACK + HELP HER BACK INTO
HER WHEELCHAIR BUT THE
BUS WAS LEAVING + RUSSLE
SAID SHE'D BE FINE.

5.15 PM
GOT OFF THE BUS EARLY + TOOK
RUSSLE TO MEAT MY GIRLFRIEND + I
CAN SHOW HER THE TTATTOO TOO! I
REMEMBERD THAT SHE WORKS LATE ON
WENSDAYS SO WE LET OURSELVES IN THRU
THE SPARE BEDROOM WINDOW. HELPED
OURSELVES TO A COUPLE OF GLASSES OF
WINE, SHE WONT MIND. THEN WE HAD A
LOOK THRU HER LAUNDARY BASKET +
TRYED SOME OF HER CLOTHES ON TO
MAKE EACH OTHER LAUGH. RUSSLE TOOK
SOME OF HER CLOTHES WITH HIM +
PROMISED HED BRING THEM BACK
NEXT TIME. I HAD ANOTHER COLD,
POWDERY CRAP + THEN WE LEFT.
RUSSLE REALY DIDNT LIKE HER CAT,
+ THE CAT DIDNT SEAM TO LIKE
HIM EITHER.

THINK I FORGOT TO FLUSH
OOPS!

LOL

7.25 P.M

RUSSLE HAS BEEN ASKING ABOUT
MY UPDATES + WHY I DO THEM.
I TOLD HIM THAT IF I DONT I FIND
IT HARD TO REMEMBER WHAT IVE DONE.
HE SAID ITS LIKE ONE OF THOUES
OLD FASHIONED DIARYS THAT PEOPLE USED
TO KEEP. HE SAID THAT THESE DAYS
PEOPLE GO ON COMPUTERS TO TELL THE
WHOLE WORLD WHAT THEY ARE DOING
BUT I DONT LIKE THE IDEA OF THAT.
HE SAID HE LIKES THE WAY I DOCUMENT
EVERYTHING I DO THRU THE DAY ON
SCRAPS OF PAPPER + STORE THEM IN
STRICKT ORDER IN HUNDREDS OF SHOUE
BOXES NEVER TO BE READ BY ANYBODY
BUT ME. I SAID HE CAN WRITE SOME
IF HE WANTS. HE SAID HE DIDNT
WANT TO.
I SAID I DIDNT WANT HIM TO READ
ANY OF THEM.

HE SAID IM NOT ALOUD TO WRITE
ABOUT HIM.

IM GOING FOR A BATH.

8·43 P.M

THERES STILL NO HOT WATER SO I
HAD TO COVER MYSELF IN MARGARINE
BEFORE I GOT IN SO I DIDNT FAINT AGAIN.
MY STOMACH STINGS. THINK I'M STARTING TO
REGRET GETTING THIS TATTOO NOW. I WAS SAT THEIR
IN THE BATH, WITH HER SCREAMING CRYING FACE
LOOKING UP AT ME + I STARTED THINKING HOW I FEEL
WHEN IM WACHING ONE OF THOUSE FILMS FROM AMERICA
+ YOU SEE THE SUN IN THE BACKGROUND + YOU REALISE THAT
ITS THE SAME SUN SHINEING THRU YOUR WINDOW, ITS THE SAME
FAMOUS SUN. BUT WHEN YOU SEE THE SUN SHINEING DOWN ON THOUSE
FAMOUS, UGLY PEOPLE IT DOSNT FEEL LIKE ITS YOUR SUN ANYMORE
BUT IT IS STILL MY SUN, NOT THERES, LIKE SHE IS STILL MINE TOO.

11·27 P.M

ITS AT THE NIGHTIME THAT I MISS
HER THE MOST. BUT RUSS IS WITH ME NOW
SO THATS O·K. I LOVE RUSSLE. HES A GOOD
BLOKE. ITS OUR FIRST EVENING TOGETHER SO
WE ATE OURSELVES A COUPLE OF BIRTHDAY CAKES
+ DRANK THE REST OF HER WINE, WACHED
COOL RUNINGS + HAD A GOOD CRY.
YOU KNOW WHAT, I THINK WE'RE GOING TO
BE JUST FINE.

THURSDAY 8.49 AM

WOKE EARLY AGAIN
+ WAS VERY PLESED
TO FIND I CAN
NOW SUCK
MYSELF OFF
DELIGHTED!

:)

10.35 AM

NO I CANT!

MUSIC FOR THE PEOPLE

Music for the people
The songs your fathers sang
Were written by their fathers
And their fathers before them
But the songs your children sing
Are written by the evil
Hands of marketeers and business men
Music for the people

Music for the people
The diet of your soul
Is woven from the fabric
Of distraction and control
It is broadcast like a church bell
Ringing from a steeple
But should be observed like an air-raid siren
Music for the people

Music for the people
Moves into my mind
Like a flushed turd
Sliding down an underground pipe
It burrows its way into my brain
Never to be removed
My head is just a mix-tape
Full of other people's tunes

Manipulating soundwaves
To create the shape of music
And the emotion it evokes
Is merely an illusion

The atmosphere created by vibrations in the room
Is just as soulless as a robot programmed to sing the Blues
It cannot stop a bullet
It will not end a war
It cannot be held responsible for you falling in love
It will not cure the weakling child
Or put an end to evil
Don't give up the day job
Music for the people

Music for the people
The forgotten art of folk
Stolen by some bearded weirdo wearing a pullover
It's not for the fashionista following a code
It's for passing information
To the generation below
"Where is your hero now?" the sleazy DJ cries
This club has been reserved for crooks and paedophiles
He pulls on the rubber glove for your initiation
"Because we can't have just anyone
Who comes along becoming famous"
And that rumbling beneath your feet
Is not a distant rave
It is the tremors of Sid Vicious
Spinning in his grave
It's the sound of the underground
Learning to obey
Staring at the radio
Doing what the DJ says

And my Argos Telecaster
That I never learnt to play
Glares at me across the bedroom
And sighs as if to say

"If you couldn't be bothered
Why on Earth should they
Make the effort of putting a smile
On your cynical face"
The only art I ever mastered
Was the art of the complaint
And my early stuff was ok
But this all just sounds the same
And nothing's ever going to change
And the reason why is simple
There is no money left to be made
Music for the people

SUPERBAD

I performed this poem for Radio 4 in 2008. When it was broadcast I noticed the line about "race horse semen" had been edited out. "The BBC are very careful about these things," I was told, which is odd because there is also a line in the poem about sodomising your mum which seemed to slip through the BBC's net. Let's see if you can spot it...

Teach your children to spend money well
I didn't listen and I ran up a bill
Someone else's money that I can't pay back
I lost a hand to a card cheat called Superbad
Would you lend money from a man
With a hook for a hand and gambler's cramp
Who daren't smile in case
He might break his poker face
Money in my pocket baby
I've got debt to pay
I went to my mother, she won't open the door
My father turns his face away and spits on the floor
I borrowed from my brother but I still can't afford it
I went to the law but they just ignored me
I heard about one man who ran a bookies shop
He ended up with a pocket full of bad luck
So Superbad tied him up in a sack
Filled with broken glass and live rats
Tied him to an anchor and he threw him in the sea
Now I'm sick with worry
Man, I can't sleep or eat
Coz I hear that Superbad is coming looking for me
High tech piracy
The treasonous business of the high seas
The man
With one hand singing pieces of hate
His name is Superbad
And he's here to take everything I own
For his own

He only stole it coz it wasn't nailed down
But if you can't steal it
He'll be wheeling and dealing it
From gold bullion to race horse semen
Pirate wild
One eye
Five fingers in twenty-five pies
A magpie sat by his side at all times
And some folks tell me that he can't die
The only place he wants to be is richer than the queen
Maybe I could wake up and it's all been a dream
But it's not that easy to get away from Superbad
He knows this town like the back of your mum's head
Dressed in a three-quarter length black coat
Decorated blood red and gold
His one good hand on his sword
He's drinking grain alcohol from a human skull
Smoking a pipe made from a bone
Filled with a spice that will get you so stoned
You'll swear you just saw your own soul
Takes you to a place that you've never been before
And you sure as hell won't want to go back there
All hands at the helm lads
I keep watching my back for Superbad
Would you follow him into battle and back?
Would you do it if he held a gun to your head?
Swift and vicious like a shark attack
Die for the name of Superbad
Sharpened teeth
Old English speech
In a cracked accent from way back
Eternal torment
He does not sleep
A gypsy put a curse on Superbad
I am told he's over 700 years old
He ate a gypsy's baby to ingest its soul

Now he's cursed by the gypsy
He can't die
You can't kill him
So don't even try
Or he'll come back like a relentless storm
Knocks you back and forth
And makes you wish that you weren't born
Take it on the chin
Take it like a man
Takes you to hell and back and afterwards say thanks
Pay your respects
Count what you've got left
And be grateful to walk away with both of your legs
Take these words with you and tell your friends
Superbad comes tomorrow and he stinks of revenge
I wrote this with a gun on the table
I thought it would bring me hope
As I wait for this vicious circle
To finally grind to a close
And I can smell him getting closer
Here comes the hand on my shoulder
Here comes the knife in my back
He ripped my skin like a rag
Kept my eyes in a bag
Threw my burnt bones to unrest on the sea bed
Threaded my teeth like jewellery beads through my own hair
Which he now wears round his neck
He swallowed my soul
He took everything that I own
I got got by

SUPERBAD...

POLITICIANS ARE LIKE POETS

Politicians are like poets
People want them to suffer for their work
We don't like to think of them as privileged
Or even happy
We want them malnourished
And on the verge of a nervous breakdown
People want politicians and poets
To have to crawl through the arsehole of life
To taste the experience first hand
But most of them haven't
So we just pretend that we have!
Lying is our very nature

Politicians are like poets
A few of them do it because they must
And I mean a handful do it because they have no choice
Because that's the hand life dealt them
For the passionate anger and love
But most of them choose to do it
Because the lifestyle appealed to them
Because they were seduced by the idea of becoming the
"Spokesman of their generation"
"The voice of the people"
And although they set out with good intentions
Thinking they would really make a difference
We all just end up getting arrested at four in the morning
Staggering round a park barefoot and coke-faced
Wearing nothing but a dressing gown and a fez

Politicians are like poets
Over-rehearsed insincere bullshitters preaching to the converted
The only people who are interested in what they have to say
Are hecklers and their own colleagues who secretly wish
They'd fuck off so they can go on after and steal their thunder

And so they stand there hogging the stage
Promoting their own self-importance
Telling everyone what they want to hear
So preoccupied with the ridiculous popularity competition
They have to have it all written down
Or else they'd forget what they're supposed to be saying

Politicians are like poets
If you've got a northern accent
You're probably not going to do that well
And if you've got a southern accent
You might want to pretend you didn't go to Eton

Politicians are like poets
All the best ones have been dead for years

Politicians are like poets
Most people haven't a clue what they are fucking talking about
And afraid of coming across stupid they'll say
"Oh, I don't know much about it, I'm not really into it"
But it's ok
Because politics is a lot like poetry
Even if you have an opinion
Everybody's going to tell you that you're wrong

Poets are a lot like politicians
Some of them are performers
Some of them (think they) are comedians
A lot of them are faceless recluses
Who think they can change your life with the stroke of a pen
And although they are annoying and creepy and very very boring
All that any of them want is for you to like them
Because politicians are a lot like poets
You wouldn't really trust them with your kids
And all of them hide behind their words

LOVE IN A SLING!

IM IN LOVE

& LOVE IS GREAT

I MAY HAVE SCARS

FROM FLYING PLATES

DAMAGED EYE SIGHT

I CANT SEE STRAIGHT

BUT IM IN HOSPITAL

& LOVE IS GREAT

The first job I had was at the Stretford Arndale discount dentist, sweeping up the teeth. On quiet shifts they'd let me do the odd filling, but I wasn't very good at it and left when I could no longer wash the smell of breath off my clothes. And so I went to work in the kitchens of Manchester with the worst people in the world. Chefs. After 18 years I left to write this book. 18 fucking years. I could have killed a couple of those chefs and served less time in prison. In the words of Philip Larkin...

"PAST SMELLS OF DIFFERENT DINNERS"

I threw in the greasy tea towel
And waved bye bye with a blistered hand
My bedroom no longer smells of chips
According to my girlfriend
The hellish iron
And fire and yelling
And sweating and wishing the shit shift would end
Has ended and never again
Will I have to ditch
Twelve litres of onion soup in the bin
Just because my blue plaster fell into it
No more red-faced lunatics
Grabbing each other by the throat
Or waitresses bursting into tears
Running home and leaving their coat
And no more saboteurs spoiling each other's
Dinners with fistfuls of salt
And the dancing
And stretching
And reaching
And bending
And leaning
And kneeling
And lying
And lending
Has ended

I used to imagine we were all performing a contemporary dance
   piece and if we removed the ovens and the tiles and the
   knives and the pans of boiling carcasses and if we swapped
   our whites for black leotards and placed us instead on a
   stage we would perform exactly the same ridiculous
   manoeuvres tightly around each other in a show that would
   last for 16 fucking hours
Ah well
Back to the chopping board

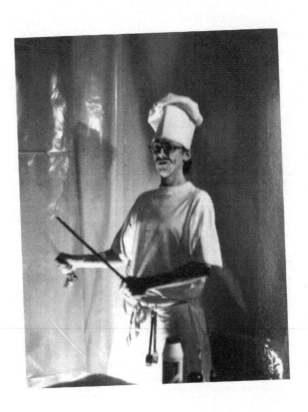

DEAD FOREVER

I've got tombstones for sale
Dig you own grave
There's plenty of space left
Bring your own spade
The undertaker looks a little bit like Tom Waits
Top hat and tails and a pale shade of grey
Points at me and he takes out a tape measure
And says that he wants to know my name
And he laughed as he carved my epitaph
It said *You're dead forever and you're never coming back*

The battle of the big bad question
The question that every man must take some time to wrestle with
But it's not the answer that scares us
It's not knowing what haunts us
Makes us lie wide-eyed awake until morning
Pull your own hair out
Pistols at dawn
Until you declare war on your own thoughts
And you only realised that you'd lost that war
When only one man rode back dead on his horse
And you buried him alone
You cried
You sang him a song and you're not sure why
Left him some flowers
And then left him for dead
Because now he's dead forever
And he's never coming back

Would you like to float around your own funeral?
Find out what people really thought about you?
Your brother didn't have a good word to say
He had your widow on his arm before they opened the buffet
Cold cuts
Paper plates

Triangular sliced grey egg mayonnaise
The mortician got a bit slap-happy with the face paint
And you ended up a shade of old lady beige
The pall-bearers are some guys you don't even know
Their poor parents are all either dead or too old
But it doesn't matter whether you're the last or the first
Of your gang to take a turn for the worst
When it's your turn to take a drive in the hearse
You've got the same things waiting for you
As they lug you into church
You're going to go through the curtains
Get burnt
Smoke like a kipper
And tipped into an urn
To rest in peace on the mantelpiece
While your mental wife worries where you've been
In your will
You asked to be thrown into the sea
Instead you ended up making a bailiff sneeze
When he picked up the telly too fast
And you went *SMASH*
You're dead forever
And you're never coming back

I only lasted in the undertakers for half a week though
I had to break a dead twelve-year old's cheek bones
With a toffee hammer
To try and take
The shocked expression of rape off her face
After rigor mortis set in
Her parents wanted an open coffin
The moment they unzipped that bag
I immediately threw up into my hands
Never smelt nothing like that before

DON'T GET A JOB IN A MORGUE!

Is life just a bowl of cherries?
Am I just a hole in the obituaries?
Or do we all have to get busy checking in to Heaven
When we're finished getting dead and buried?
Am I just a zombie waiting to happen
Or will I live again
Like Peter Frampton?
I hit the bottle like a heavyweight champion
And ponder how long until I turn into a skeleton
Because it can't just be nothing
That can't be right
Because when I close my eyes I can still see a light
But there'll be no light when that switch gets flicked
And I can't picture a more vivid abyss
I'm talking about NOTHING
Nothing to fear
Nothing to worship
As far as I'm aware there isn't even a word for it
Because there'll be no words
No light
No thought
No time
No space
And nothing to record it
So when faced with death
We should learn to laugh
Because once it's happened
There's no coming back
We should all just relax
And enjoy it while it lasts
Because we'll all be dead forever
And we're never coming back

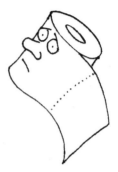

I CAN SEE YOU

You come rolling home at 5 in the morning
With the stink of the South on your clothes
Your face has been in each tabloid newspaper today
I'm surprised you've not died of exposure
And again you won't sleep
Your insecurities
Come screaming from out of the hole
That paranoid void in the centre of you
That cocaine just doesn't quite fill

Don't try to smile
It just doesn't work
Your eyes are too insincere
And that grimacing shape that you make with your face
Looks more like an expression of fear
Are you afraid that somebody might see you
And find out you're not who you appear
Well I can see you
And you look like a child that's about to burst into tears

Do you wish you could just walk away from it all
Curl up in a ball
Disappear
Well we all wish you would
So why don't you just fuck off
No one even knows why you're here
It would appear you're apparently famous for something
But what that might be isn't clear
Feels like I've been trapped in a lift with you
For the past five bastard years

There's a party tonight
You'll get out of your mind
Fall out of the taxi and into the frying pan

Let your eyes roll back into your
Hedonistic life
On the edge of a knife
Tense as a tightrope
When did you last laugh out loud?
Your mood swings sway with the weight of a thunder cloud
Your parents pushed you through Brit School
So don't pull that face when the next hoop you jump through
Has been set on fire
And you change your mind
And your management drop you
Like your last hot rock
That landed on your crotch
And burns a hole through your pride

Why must we only use money and fame
To measure somebody's success?
If you can't learn to sail on life's ups and downs
You will never feel content
And you expect me to feel sympathy
Because you're lonely and depressed
Well it's no fucking wonder when your life's as hollow
As a bleeding Easter Egg
No it's no fucking wonder when your life's as shallow
As the pie filling at Greggs

I've seen newer material in Oxfam

I've seen more edge in a U2 tribute band

Your word is as reliable as an orphan's Christmas wish

To me you are uglier than a council-funded graffiti mural

You're more full of shit than the kitchen drawer

Drug-induced paranoid schizophrenia?
Even the voices in your head stop talking to you
Because you're such an intolerable bastard

I can see through you like Clark Kent could see through
Lois Lane's dress
Fame's what you wish for
Fame's what they gave you
And you've only been paid in regret
So don't forget
The next time you stare inanely down that camera lens
I can see you

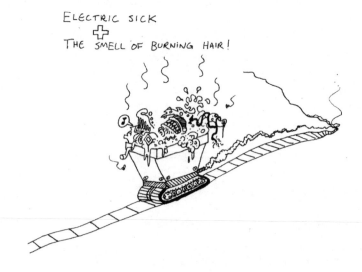

THE 'ORRIBLE MILE

For Dave Roberts, R.I.P.

Cigarettes for breakfast again
Woke up and didn't know where I was
Picked myself up
Dusted myself down
And I hitchhiked onto a truck
The driver's name was Tony
He chain-smoked
And he took far too much speed
He sounded so Mancunian he was almost Scouse
And he drove faster than I speak
I asked Tony where he was going
He said he had to get out of town
Said he's going to lay low in a local shithole he knows
Called the 'orrible mile
And we arrived in the middle of the night
In this piss wet seaside town
We found a shitty little bed and breakfast
And we got our heads down for a couple of hours
And the following day
We robbed the old lady who ran that B&B
And that night we hit the town so hard
We put a crack down the side of the pier
Twelve pints of black stuff
Two bags of white stuff
Three and a half boxes of red
Flashing the cash with panache you bastard
I thought I was Mr. Cigarettes
The weekender bender to remember
We blew the money in one night
But the merry-go-round
It broke down
And now we're stranded on the 'orrible mile

Couldn't remember where we parked the truck
We didn't see it for another three days
So for the time being we have to make ends meet
Picking pockets in the penny arcade
And all the money that we made
We gambled it away
Hit the jackpot once or twice
But we must have been kicked out of every fucking casino
Up and down the 'orrible mile
Protection
Get yourselves a weapon
These streets are paved with piss
Most of the folks round these parts
Don't even know what a policeman is
There's a bookies
A bailiffs
An undertakers
A brothel
And a bar
There are only fives ways you can earn a wage
When you're working on the 'orrible mile
Look out for the lady with the pout and the paint
Trying to call you in up off the streets
I saw a nun strip down to how God intended
With a twenty dollar note in her teeth
But if you need to get laid
Leave your name and your number
I'll be back in touch within the half an hour
But don't say I didn't warn you
You'll run screaming down the 'orrible mile
I fell for a fallen lady
With a fake name and a vicious lust
It was a stupid arrangement
Based on payment
The closest I came to love
She suggested that I wear a blindfold

And then she robbed me blind
And with one bare foot I had to walk all the way
Back up the 'orrible mile
Maybe I'm going soft
But something in me is screaming to go
I'd burnt every bridge I've crossed
I think I'd better get my coat
But I left my pride behind
Kind of felt like part of me's died
The street lights came on as I walked past them
Goodbye 'orrible mile
But Tony stayed there a little too long
He caught the needle fever after a while
And the last I'd heard he's turned nocturnal
Now he only comes out at night
But Tony told me moths are simply ghosts of butterflies
Well I suppose that you can't
Be afraid of the dark
When you're living on the 'orrible mile

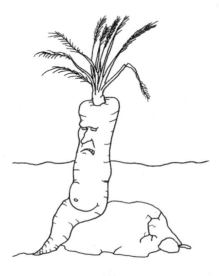

TEMPORARY TOURETTE'S

Temporary Tourette's
The totally spontaneous pre-meditated verbal outburst
Temporary Tourette's
The carefully selected highly inappropriate appropriate words
We're all grown ups
So let's just see how far we can lower the tone
Temporary Tourette's
Stuck in your throat like a tracheotomy blow job
Language is a massive part of our lives
But we're tied by the binds of being polite
Freedom of speech ain't all it's cracked up to be
So why not allow it to become a blessing in disguise
There are so many words to say
To convey the anger and pleasure and sadness and pain
And sooner or later one of these days
You will have to face up to everything you're afraid of
So just remember that the brutal truth
Is always more important than some bullshit excuse

Second verse, worse than the first
It's just an onslaught of vicious slurs and curse words
A spoon full of venom makes the medicine burn
The most inappropriate appropriate words
Temporary Tourette's
The intention of causing offence
You are the biggest pair of beef curtains since Deirdre Barlow's neck
You are the biggest bell-end since the back of Darth Vader's head
You sphincter sucking
Scrotum juggling
Jiz guzzling
Urethra fucking
Tit blister
Sister fister
Dick sneeze

Arse vinegar
Fanny hammer
Wotsit cock [3]
Massive flaccid phallus
Like a boneless obese baby's arm
Clit slit
I can't believe it's nut butter
Predator's lips [4]
Tool tuggery
Skull fuckery
Dead baby animal buggery
As haunting and as rancid as a thunderous posthumous queef
From a recently deceased elderly lady
(Oh fucking hell I'm sorry! You didn't want to hear that. I didn't
    want to write it either. This is a poem about censorship and
    this is exactly the reason why we need effective censorship I
    suppose. And if this poem is offensive to anybody it's offensive
    to people with Tourette's. It's a common misconception that
    it only manifests itself in swear words and I'm sure it must be
    a very difficult condition to live with. But you know, sticks and
    stones may break my bones, hows about I bum you with an
    empty glass bottle of wine and stamp on your stomach you

MASSIVE MASTURBATING BASTARDS!

(Oh god I'm so so sorry you had to read that, just imagine
how I feel writing it! Christ, my mum's got a copy of this
book! And my kids are always asking if they can look at it!
Oh god I'm so so terribly terribly sorry!) Sorry.)

But the point I'm making is
If we all have the potential to be offended
Why should this lead to anybody being censored
Because they're not trying to do it to hide it from your fragile eyes
They're not trying to protect your innocent mind
They are lying to you
And they abuse the truth to keep it from the millions
That they've been murdering people and abusing children

That is the only information that they are trying to protect
And it's by far the most offensive thing so far that I've said
But we're all too side-tracked to even notice it
Because we couldn't smell bullshit
If they rubbed our fucking noses in it
"Oh, so you're saying that the country's being run
By a bunch of murderous pig fucking paedophiles?
I think I'd better check that with Google"
Don't be naïve!!
Manipulated information is way more offensive
Than any scattergorically constructed sentence
They are lying to you
And the brutal truth
Is always more important than some bullshit excuse
So if you only came here to hear what you wanted to hear
Edit your own words and cover your own ears
Because the truth will out
The truth shouts
The truth swears
It offends and who cares?
Temporary Tourette's

---

[3] A "Wotsit cock" is a small prawn-shaped cheesy penis that leaves a mysterious orange dust on the fingers.

[4] "Predator's lips" is a fearsome looking flange with tusks and a deep booming laugh.

THE SOUND OF ONE FAN CLAPPING.

MY IMAGINARY MANAGER SHOWBIZZ JEFF GOT ME A
SLOT AT THE EDDING-BRU FRINDGE. I HAD NOUT
BETTER TO DO SO THOUGHT 'WHY THE FUCK NOT.'
I PACKED MY...

   EMERGENCY PANTS ✓
   A LITER OF HIGH COMMISIONER ✓
   12 LOVES OF SOREEN ✓
   A LUMP OF MIGRAINE RESIN ✓
   MY FAVORATE STRANGLEING GLOVES ✓
   BOG ROLL ✓
   A VIZ ✓
   A FLASK OF BOVRIL ✓
   THIS PAPPER + THIS PEN ✓
   AND A SMALL SHEET OF ALICE IN WONDERLAND
   FLAVOR 24 HOUR MICRO-DOT ACID ✓

LOOKING BACK THIS MIND BENDINGLY POWERFULL
HALUCINOGEN WAS THE WORST POSSIBLE DRUG I COULD
HAVE TAKEN TO THE WORLD FAMOUS, MONTH LONG
THEARTRE + COMEDY FESTIVAL! BUT WE LIVE + WE
LEARN.
MY IMAGINARY MANAGER SHOWBIZZ JEFF IS A NERVOUS
DRIVER SO THE MORNING OF THE DAY BEFORE WE LEFT
HE STARTED DRINKING HEVELY TO STEDY HIS HAND.
THIS IRESPONSIBLE PRECAUTION WORKED IN OUR FAVOR
AS WE SPED THRU THE TRAFFIC LIKE GREECED LAXATIVE.
BUT SOMEWHRE NEAR CARLILE MY IMAGINARY MANAGER
SHOWBIZZ JEFF SWERVED TO AVOID HITTING A GHOST.
THE CAR BUCKED LIKE A MULE, FLIPED MID AIR LIKE A
PANCAKE, HIT THE ROAD LIKE A METEOR + WE STARTED
TO ROLL.   .

2 DAYS LATER WE ARIVED IN EDDING-BRU IN A
ROLLING CAR, WICH CONVENIETLY GROUND TO A
HALT JUST OUTSIDE THE VENUE. I PEELED MYSELF
FREE FROM THE CONSETTINA CAR WRECK, MY COAT
WAS ALL RIPPED, MY GLASSESS HAD SMASHED + I WAS
COVERD IN BOVRIL BUT REDDY FOR THE SHOW.
'MUST DASH JEFF' I SAID 'IM ON IN 5!'
BUT SHOWBIZZ JEFF WAS CLEARLY DEAD. I DUEFULLY
DOFFED MY TATTY HAT FOR A MUINETS SADDNESS +
THEN PEGGED IT INSIDE LEAVING POOR SHOWBIZZ
JEFF WITHOUT A PROPPER BURIAL.
MY IMAGINARY MANEGER THE LATE SHOWBIZZ JEFF HAD
THE LAST LAUGH THOUGE, AS BEFORE HE DIED HE HAD
FAILED TO TELL ME THAT MY UNPAID SET COULD BE NO
LONGER THAN 59 SECONDS, SQUEEZED INBETWEEN
CELEBRATED DRAG ACT LYDIA HIRST-MACDONALD + A
BARE CHESTED, CRYING PREFORMANCE ARTIST KNOWN AS
JACK GALEREUX (APARENTLY A PROTEGE OF THE MYTICAL
BOB MOYLER) FOLLOWED BY A HEVELY PREGNANT BURLESQUE
DANCER CALLED JEMIMA NIGHTIME. THEY WAS A BARE
FOOT ACUSTIC ACT WHOSE FETHERWEIGHT, NON DESCRIPT
NOODLEING WAS SO VAUGE SHE BLENDED LIKE A CHAMELION
AGAINST THE BACKDROP CURTIAN HALF WAY THRU HER
SET + WAS NEVER SEEN AGAIN. SISTER MISTLETOE
THE WORLDS STRONGEST NUN, APARENTLY SHE COULD
CARRY ANYTHING (EXEPT A CHILD!) THE COCAINE FUILLED
COMEDY OF A MILLION MID 20'S MEN WHOS NAMES I HAVE
DILLIBRETLY FORGOTEN. A VENTRILOQUIST WHO TALKS
WITH A LISP + A PUPPET ON HIS FIST WITH HALITOSIS

SURLEY THE MAJICIAN, WHO COULD PRODUE GOLD
WHATCHES OUT OF THIN AIR, MUST BE LIVING IN HIS
CAR OUT OF CHOICE. 'THE WORST GIG IN THE WORLD'
AS IT WAS BILLED WAS HOSTED BY A SHAKEING, CHAIN
SMOKEING ELDERLY MAN WHO HAD BEEN KICKED IN
THE BALLS BY THE AUDIENCE SO OFFTEN HIS CROTCH
WAS IN HIS CHIN, LIKE A MISSTER MAN.
THE ALICE IN WONDERLAND MICRO DOTS HAD STARTED
TAKEING THEYE PRICKELY GRIP WHEN HE CALLED
MY NAME + I WALKED ON STAGE. AS THE WRINKLED
GEZZER PASSED ME THE MIC HE WISHED ME LUCK
AND SAID
'WHATS THE SOUND OF ONE FAN CLAPPING?'

WHO'S BEEN EATING MY PORRIDGE?

Who's been eating my porridge?
Who's rained on my parade?
Who's pissed on my chips?
Who sunk my battleship?
Shit!
It's Thick Richard
The worst thing since unsliced bread
Stop crying
Like I've just shot your dog and shagged your dad
I've just rearranged my room
So I have to get out the wrong side of bed
EVERY DAY!
I'm too tired to smile
So piss off you clown
Who's been eating my porridge?

They say that when you're in London
You're never more than three feet away from a rat
Well when you're in Manchester
You're never more than three feet away from a dickhead
The world would be a much safer place to live in
If they just put common sense in the curriculum
The F word isn't funny
It's FUCK
Who's been eating my porridge?

Life is like a box of chocolates
There's usually a diagram on the inside of the lid
Indicating as to what's what
So why don't you just fuck off
And fuck off while you're at it
Smell the cheese!
And pick the bones out of this one you cocksuckers

I look like Harry Potter
Jarvis Cocker
Sue Perkins
And your little brother
All rolled up into one little bitter ball of gobshite
So don't tell me about it
I don't wanna hear it
I've just lost all of my poetry spirit
Who's been eating my porridge?

Angry young man?
I make Sid Vicious look like Sid Little
It's like my grandma used to say
"If you haven't got anything worth saying...